Snapchat Marketing

How to Make Snapchat Effective for Your Brand

(How to Skyrocket Your Business Through Snapchat Marketing)

Aaron McLaren

Published By **Ryan Princeton**

Aaron McLaren

Snapchat Marketing: How to Make Snapchat Effective for Your Brand (How to Skyrocket Your Business Through Snapchat Marketing)

ISBN 978-1-77485-743-4

Legal & Disclaimer

The information contained in this ebook is not designed to replace or take the place of any form of medicine or professional medical advice. The information in this ebook has been provided for educational & entertainment purposes only.

The information contained in this book has been compiled from sources deemed reliable, and it is accurate to the best of the Author's knowledge; however, the Author cannot guarantee its accuracy and validity and cannot be held liable for any errors or omissions. Changes are periodically made to this book. You must consult your doctor or get professional medical advice before using any of the suggested remedies, techniques, or information in this book.

Upon using the information contained in this book, you agree to hold harmless the Author from and against any damages, costs, and expenses, including any legal fees potentially resulting from the application of any of the

TABLE OF CONTENTS

Introduction

Have you ever thought of learning how to master the app Snapchat? Now and into the near time, Snapchat is expected to add millions of new users. Some predict the app will eventually be able to surpass Facebook or Twitter to become the top social media platforms. According to my mind, Snapchat is the future for social media, as well as marketing, and I believe companies will catch to this fact very soon.

This book is a guide to social media, too in the sense of how it impacts our lives as well as business. Understanding the social media landscape from the bottom from the beginning is crucial and you'll need to keep an eye on it prior to getting deep into the intricacies of Snapchat and other similar apps.

At the end of this book, you'll be able to comprehend the advantages of using social media for marketing and also how to utilize it effectively. Social media is about connecting and participation and fulfils a number of our biggest psychological desires.

Learn more about the reason and how social media marketing began as well as how to apply the information we have learned to our advantage.

Let's begin!

Chapter 1: Social Media Marketing

For example, in the context of the use of social media in marketing community groups are involved in many different things to address issues that are important to them. An organization that fights hunger may advocate for breakfasts for children at no cost and a boost in funding of WIC (Women and infant children) as well as more child-friendly laws from the state senators. To achieve each of these objectives the group must spring into action with letters-writing campaigns as well as direct lobbying and advertisements in the media, to name the few. Many thousands of small details and the hard work of numerous people are typically required to make a successful campaign.

When viewed from a different point of view However, it all comes to one point. The underlying principle of the organization's efforts is a single principle that is to alter people's behaviour. This is not just true for a child-hunger campaign and for any health or community development program. A group against violence would like people to cease doing violence. Teen pregnancy initiatives aim to end kids having children. An organization that promotes peace hopes for a day when peace on earth is more than a pleasant card for the holidays. This idea of changing behavior in people is the base of the principles social marketing seeks to accomplish. It seeks to improve the perception of people so that their concentration can be directed toward the specific aspect of a topic or product. It usually appeals to people's emotional beliefs and personal thinking that reflect the image of the product.

What, precisely, do you mean by social-marketing? In the Social Marketing Report, it's defined as "the application of marketing techniques used in commercials to social issues." It's the ability to apply the same principles employed in the sale of goods--such as television shows, shoes pizza, or shoes--to persuade individuals to change their behaviour. What exactly does this mean? In lieu of selling hamburgers it's selling a life free of heart attacks. Instead of convincing teens to purchase blue jeans you're convincing them the benefits of postponing their pregnancy. However, when sell blue jeans, you're still trying to influence behaviour--you're convincing people to wear jeans to feel comfortable, or for aesthetics, or even for the worth. So , what's the distinction between social or commercial advertising? Commercial marketing attempts to alter people's behaviour to the advantage of the marketer. social marketing seeks to change people's behaviour to benefit consumers, or society in general.

The steps involved in social marketing

Note down the behavior you would like to change (for example, to increase the number of mothers who receive prenatal care).

Choose your target group: What behavior do you wish to alter? You may are trying to alter the behaviour of multiple groups. In that situation, you could be able be able to affect them various ways that will bring close to the behavior you want them to adopt. The groups that are affected are typically divided, or separated by age, gender and education level or race.

• Identify the obstacles to change. Using interviews and survey, discussion groups, or different methods. You'll need to determine the factors that make it difficult or undesirable for individuals to make these changes. Are pregnant women uncomfortable in the clinic or do they feel like they're a burden when they speak about their doctor? Are the facilities too remote? Do they have to take time off from their work?

* Remove the obstacles to making changes. Develop strategies to make the process simpler, easier to access, and more appealing. Are there ways to make the clinic open for longer hours? Do nurses and physicians get more educated to discuss issues with women? This can be taken one step further. The organization could offer incentives to make (and lasting) modifications. Mothers who visit the clinic frequently throughout their pregnancy could be eligible for coupons to get free baby food, as an instance.

Try your plan on just a few people. You can then adjust your strategy based on your outcomes.

* Make known the benefits of changeand initiatives to facilitate the process more easy in a manner that encourages people to participate in your efforts. Inform people about the things you're doing to assist them. The most effective program on the planet won't be effective if the people who use it don't be aware of it. Also, they should be aware of the change in behavior. The woman expecting a baby will desire to do what is most beneficial for her baby however, she might not realize that she requires more iron during pregnancy. It's up to you and your company to inform her.

Social Marketing and advertising

A lot of people mistake social marketing with one of its elements advertising. The leaves are however only one aspect of the tree, even when they're the only thing visible. In the same way, advertising is an essential component in social media marketing however it's only a small part.

Are you confused? Take a look at the following message:

* "This is your brain taking substances," said the Partnership for a Drug-Free America's commercial some time ago when they were picturing eggs frying on a hot skillet. This was a memorable ad however, if this was all the Partnership did that would not be considered social marketing.

* "Don't do anything to harm Texas," was a popular anti-litter campaign that was well-known in the state. If the ad was aired with no any additional trash cans set up around in the entire state or being directed at a particular population groups who reside in Texas (such as teenagers or foreigners, or immigrants) the ad was simply an attractive slogan. It would not have been social marketing.

* Smokey Bear and his message, "Only you can prevent forest fires" in the absence of T.V., are

again simply an advertisement. When viewed in relation to the entire work carried out through the U.S. Forestry Service, what emerges is a campaign for social media. Smokey is trying to alter one particular habit (being negligent using fire) His message is targeted to the right group of people (six to ten years old) and the information that he offers (on commercials as well as through the Internet and in other places) will overcome two main obstacles for children to be cautious around fire: ignorance, and the scientific "it's not fun" hurdle. Furthermore the message is backed with the information that parents receive at camping sites and campgrounds, which makes it more likely they will be able to reinforce the message. This is called social marketing. It utilizes targeted marketing, reinforcement, and it lowers obstacles. Three key elements are missing from the two examples previously mentioned.

Credibility and the importance of social Marketing

The problem is that there's an art to it. It's not the stuff you're born with and it's more than just common sense. There are people who earn degrees in this field major companies like Nike or Coca-Cola invest billions of dollars to ensure their marketing campaigns are of the latest technology. This is why, in the review, it was mentioned that the ability to market relies on the creative mind of an individual and abilities. The good news is first of all it's a trait that can be learned. It's possible that you weren't born with terms like market segmentation floating in your brain, but you are able to discover what they mean and then use them in your own business.

Second, it's scalable. Certain campaigns are massive for example, like that of the National High Blood Pressure campaign. However social marketing campaigns may also be a little smaller. This means that you can implement it locally even when you're limited in resources. Even if your organization isn't running in the same way as the Hyatt Regency, or hasn't resources that are that is comparable but that doesn't mean that you won't be able to apply the same ideas and implement the change you'd like to be able to see within your local community.

Three major benefits which suggest that the concept of social marketing is worthy of review:

It allows you to reach those you wish to get to.

* It allows you to tailor your message to the right audience segments; and in doing this, you can reach out to them.

* It assists in creating an even longer-lasting and lasting change in behavior for those groups.

The concept of social marketing can be a smart idea as it can be effective.

Fundamental Marketing Principles

Before we get into discussing social marketing in more detail However, it's essential to be aware of the fundamentals of commercial marketing, as it's what the concept is based on. As health professionals in the community, or even members of non-profit organisations it might appear strange. We're accustomed to a different perspective. The words "marketing" might conjure images of corporate and big business greed, but they don't inspire us to think of programs to aid our fellow citizens.

But, even so you may find that your neighbors won't agree with your suggestions and strategies right away And you might be required to convince them. That's what social marketing is a master in. The concept may be novel for you, or it could be a radical change in how you think about things. The change could be the fresh air your business needs to become even more efficient in changing the way it conducts business.

The fundamentals of marketing can be summarized into what's known as"the "4 four Ps." These are the product, price location, promotion, and price.

* Product The product is the thing you're marketing. Social marketing's "product" can be a specific way of life you're trying to alter. It could include ending the abuse of children and neglect and preventing suicides from happening or convincing people not litter the ground, or any other behaviour that people in your community are looking to alter.

Prices -- What is it going to cost someone to end (or to adopt) an action? In the world of social marketing, price isn't just about cents and dollars. It could be also a matter about time (i.e. what time does it take me to locate the trash bin?) or the amount of a commitment a alteration will take. If you're a smoker for a long time, you could be the first to acknowledge that smoking cigarettes is a very expensive habit yet they might still believe the expenses--in terms and weight gain or withdrawal from nicotine. He just can't quit.

A sound social marketing strategy is then able to lower the cost of these services. A campaign against litter will attempt to increase the number of trash bins throughout the city. A smoking cessation organization could offer assistance groups to aid in the journey, nutrition counselling to help prevent weight gain and nicotine patches that can lessen the withdrawal symptoms.

* Location -What is the difficulty to modify the behavior? What obstacles hinder from doing so? If you're making blue jeans available, it is important to be able to offer them in stores all across the nation and not just one tiny boutique situated in Snellville, Georgia. If not, those who live in Oregon aren't capable of purchasing them, even if they'd like to.

Also, if you're "selling" the prevention of teenage pregnancy What obstacles make it difficult to stop these pregnancy? Are teens able to easily access birth control pills, or is it difficult to obtain it? There might not be a reliable teenage clinic in the town. If there is an available clinic, perhaps it's across town, but it's only open during the week from 8:00 to 4:00. It's difficult to access without having to miss school.

Social marketing makes it easier to influence behaviors by making sure that the appropriate supports are not only accessible, but accessible to the largest number of people who are able to benefit. The less people have to be pushed to take a step towards change and the more likely they will be to be able to do the change.

* Promotion * Promotion final one of the "4 Ps," and the one that is most commonly linked to social marketing. Promotion is the type of advertising you use, be it in commercials on television or in letters to editors, or red ribbons that are tied to automobile antennas.

Promoting your cause does not have to cost a lot of cash. It can be accomplished with less costly strategies like the old-fashioned way of spreading word-of-mouth. The ability to convince people via a one-on one conversation is as effective in altering the perspective of someone as the most well-crafted commercial, or more. (Think over it. What could trigger you to take an injection of tetanus: a commercial on TV or a suggestion from your physician?) The power of word-of mouth advertising is a popular aspect of social media marketing.

The Stages of an Effective Social Marketing Strategy

With this understanding of marketing with us, let's shift our focus towards the main focus of any successful campaign: the customer. Different people will have different opinions and opinions at different time. For instance, among smokers there are those who do not believe smoking cigarettes is bad for their health, while others may be aware of the dangers, but may not be concerned while others might not be willing to make the step of quitting smoking, while a last group of smokers might be actively seeking to stop. Social marketing campaigns look at all these views (and their associated actions) as parts of a continuum and attempt to help individuals to the next stage.

The concept is that the changes won't be a quick process. The majority of people will not go from believing that smoking is "cool" but not aware of the health risks, to stopping smoking right away. In fact, a social media marketing campaign may get people thinking that quitting smoking isn't the best choice. after the thought has had time to flip around in their minds for some time, another aspect of the program will assist to stop smoking, while another component will help them stay smoke-free.

What are the factors that influence these beliefs and what are the decisions that are made? In general the following actions need to happen:

* Increase awareness and stimulate interest

"Change attitudes, conditions and attitude

* Inspire people to change their behaviour

• Empower people to take action

* Avoid the possibility of backsliding

Examples of Stages that have been Successful

In a lot of Africa women have traditionally been blessed with many children. In some countries such as Nigeria where the average woman could have as many as 12 children in her lifetime. One of the social marketing messages that has been widely spread and promoted is that women should having fewer children. The message has been designed toward the goal of improving women's healthand reducing the number of children and food insecurity.

* Create awareness and arouse interest. The person receiving the message in a literal way. It is imperative to grab the attention of the person. The message must be communicated to women across the nation, including the village

women who are typically ineducated, only speak local dialects and often do not have access to radio or television. Additionally, the person receiving the message must be able to understand the message. The message does not only must be delivered to women in a language that they can comprehend, but it must have a meaning to their lives too. For women living in Africa their status and wealth have been traditionally tied with the number of children they have. The notion of having less children isn't an option because it could adversely affected their status in the society, even though it improved their health.

* Refuse to accept the conditions and attitudes. The person who is receiving the gift must develop an optimistic attitude or mental attitude towards the conduct that is being questioned. Through effective social marketing, African women might come to the conclusion that "Maybe it's better to have less children."

* Inspire people to alter their behavior. The person who is receiving the message must form an intention to take action based on this mindset. It's not enough just to convince people that an idea is good. It's necessary to take a leap taken from the idea that it's an "good suggestion" to the point of "I will try this." Think

about it this way: how many of us believe it's a beneficial idea to cut back on our consumption of fats or rise at 5 a.m. to work out? Social marketing can help people go from attitude to action and even beyond. If you're an African ladies, that could involve taking the plunge to discover more about birth control options or plan to delay sexual relations.

The ability to empower people to take action. The person receiving the gift must take action, i.e., convert the desire into an action. The woman or the person with whom she is must visit the clinic, and obtain the birth control pill, and to make use of it.

• Prevent backsliding. Most of the time, the action of the recipient is followed by reinforcement, or providing some reward for the action, so that the desired behavior will be repeated. What can she do to improve her life by having less children? Do her family and friends get better? Are there more funds? Do she have the ability to go to school? Are they healthier than their neighbours?

We've already mentioned that there aren't all people at the same point in the continuum. It's as if they're in different places on the bridge, which spans from awareness to action.

Social marketing is an idea that's relatively new to the health and development industry. However, it's a concept that has great potential, and could provide you with the perfect framework to ensure that your business can achieve the things you've decided to achieve: helping individuals and the entire society to live healthier lives. Modern business markets have an important role to play in promotional activities for businesses in the field of Social Marketing in such a extremely competitive market. With the advancement of technology today it is not wise not to make use of these advancements to promote products on a larger scale. Social marketing is a key component and the area it's most utilized for is through social media. This is the reason why it was born Social Media Marketing.

Chapter 2: Social Media Marketing Platforms

The term "social media marketing," also known as SMM is a kind of internet-based marketing that uses diverse social media platforms in order to reach goals of branding and communication. Social media marketing typically covers actions that involve social sharing of videos, articles and photos to promote marketing and also paid social media ads. The majority of social media platforms feature built-in analytics tools for data that allow companies to monitor the progress, effectiveness and effectiveness of their ads. Social media marketing campaigns typically concentrate on the creation of content that draws attention and encourages users to share the content with the social media networks they use. Corporate messages are spread across users and is likely to be a hit since it is believed to originate from a trustworthy third-party source in contrast to the company or brand. This type of marketing is based on word-of-mouth. This generates earned media instead of paid media. Social media has evolved into an internet-based platform that is accessible to everyone who has access to the internet. A greater level of communication between organizations can lead to branding and, often better customer service. Furthermore, social media functions as a cost-effective option for businesses to execute marketing campaigns. Businesses can reach a variety of stakeholder groups through social media marketing, including current and prospective customers, potential and current employees journalists, bloggers as well as the public at large. At a strategic level the social media marketing process includes the management of the execution of a campaign for marketing and governance, defining the goals (e.g. more active or less passive use) and the development of the company's"standards" for social media "culture" as well as its "tone". To make use of social media effectively firms must be able to permit customers as well as Internet users to share content created by users (e.g. online reviews, comments or product reviews, etc.) Also called "earned media" instead of using advertisements written by marketers. Although it is usually associated with businesses however, as of the year 2016, many not-for-profits and government entities are using social media for marketing for their programs or services.

Social Media Marketing Platforms

Social networks allow individuals business, as well as other organizations to connect with each other and form communities and relationships online. If companies sign up to these networks, users are able to communicate directly with them. The interaction may be more personal for consumers as opposed to traditional techniques of advertising and outbound marketing. Social networks act as word of mouth , or more precisely, e-word of mouth. The ability of the Internet to connect billions of people across the globe has provided internet-based word of mouth a strong voice with a vast reach. The capability to quickly alter buying habits and patterns of services acquisition and activities to an increasing number of customers is referred to by the term influence networks. Blogs and social networking sites permit followers to "retweet" as well as "repost" messages posted by other people about a product or service being promoted. This happens frequently on certain social media platforms. Through repetition users' connections can see the message and thus reach many more people. Because details about the product are being shared and getting repeated, more people are attracted to the product or company.

Social networks are built on creating virtual communities that permit users to share their desires wishes, values and wants on the internet. Social media marketing connects these people and their audiences to companies that have the same wants, needs and beliefs. Through social networks businesses can stay contact with their individual users. Personal interactions can bring an impression of loyalty in the followers as well as potential customers. Furthermore, by choosing which people you follow through these websites they can help brands have a limited market. Social networks also provide many details about the services and products potential clients may want to know about. With the help of modern techniques for semantic analysis marketers can identify buying signals such as posts shared by users and online questions. A better understanding of the buying signals can assist salespeople target prospects who are relevant and marketers create micro-targeted marketing campaigns.

In order to integrate social media in their marketing strategies, businesses must develop an effective marketing strategy. A model of marketing that is based on social networks, a model is available. The model comprises these steps

* Selecting the possible social networks to utilize;

* Creating the budget (regarding the hiring of social media consultant or brand manager);

* Redesigning or changing organizational structures in order to manage the social media networks in the market of the company (this could involve the addition of a social media department to the existing marketing branch or even establishing a brand separate social media department);

* Selection of markets to target;

* The selection of the products or services, brands, or corporate messages that will be promoted

* Performance measures to support your social media plan, such as data analytics, evaluation, etc.

In 2014, more than 80 percent of business leaders recognized social media as an essential part in their businesses. Retailers have experienced 133% growth in their revenue due to marketing via social media.

Social Media Marketing Strategies

There are two fundamental methods to engage with the social media for marketing:

Passive Approach

Social media is an effective source of market information as well as an opportunity to listen to the opinions of customers. Content communities, blogs forums, and blogs are all platforms which allow people to post their comments and suggestions for brands products, services, and brands. Businesses can study and interpret the customer opinions and feedback that are generated on social media to promote their products and services and in this regard, social media are an low-cost source of market information that can be utilized by managers and marketers to identify and address the issues that consumers have identified and also to spot potential market opportunities. For instance it was the case that the Internet was flooded with images and videos of iPhone 6 "bend test" which proved that the highly-coveted phone was able to bend under the pressure of a hand. The"bend gate" or "bend gate" controversy has caused confusion among users who had waited for months to see the latest version of the iPhone. The company, however, Apple promptly issued a statement that said the issue was very rare and the company took a variety of steps to make the case more durable and sturdy. In contrast to traditional methods of market research like focus groups, surveys and data mining, which cost a lot of time and money and can could take months or even weeks to analyse, marketers can make use of social media to get "live" and "real time" information on the behavior of consumers and their opinions on the company's products or brand. This can be extremely useful in the dynamic global, fast-paced, and competitive market of the decade of 2010.

Active Approach

Social media is used not just for public relations or direct marketing tools, but also channels for communication that target very specific groups of people through social media influencers as well as social media personalities, and as tools to engage customers. Social media-related technologies that predate social media such as broadcast television as well as newspapers, also offer advertisers a targeted audience, since ads placed on broadcast of a sports event or in the section on sports in the newspaper will likely be read by avid sports fans. Yet, these sites can target niche markets more specifically. Utilizing digital tools, such as Google Ad-Sense, advertisers can tailor their advertisements to specific segments of the population, like people who are interested political activism, social entrepreneurship related to a specific social party or even video gaming. Google Ad-Sense does this by seeking out keywords in users' blog posts as well as comments. It's difficult for a television station or newspaper to offer ads that are so targeted (though it is not impossible as observed in "special special" sections that focus on specific issues that newspapers could use to market specific advertisements).

However, there are some ways that a business can take to improve its social image and to promote its brand via the use of social media for marketing.

1. Establish your business Goals

Every element in your digital marketing plan helps you achieve the goals you've have set. It's impossible to make progress without knowing what you're aiming for.

Take a close look at your business's requirements in general and then decide the best way to utilize social media in the goals of your business.

There's a good chance that you'll develop a list of your own goals however there are some which all businesses should incorporate in their strategies: increasing awareness of their brand retention of customers and reducing the cost of marketing are important to all. I suggest that you select two main goals and two secondary objectives to concentrate on. If you have too many goals, it will distract you and you'll ultimately achieve nothing.

2. Create Marketing Goals

They're not very useful when you don't have precise conditions that specify the time when each goal is met. For instance If one of your main goals is to generate lead and revenue, what is the does it take to generate the number of leads as well as sales you need to achieve before you think that your goal has been achieved?

Marketing objectives outline how you go from the point A (an unfulfilled target) towards Point B (a successful achievement of the target). It is possible to determine your goals using the S-M-A-R T approach to make your goals specific that are measurable, feasible, pertinent and time-bound.

In the previous example, If your objective is to create sales and leads and leads, one of your marketing objectives might be to boost leads by 50 percent. To track your progress, decide which tracking and analytics tools you'll need in the first place. Set yourself up for the possibility of failure is never an excellent idea. If you have set a goal to increase sales 1000 percent, it's unlikely that you'll achieve the target. Make sure you set goals you can reach with the resources available. You've had the opportunity to make your goals more precise so they're appropriate to your company So, extend that thought to your goals. If you'd like to receive the support of your top executives make sure your goals are in line with the overall mission of your company.

The adherence of a timeline to your efforts is crucial. What time do you expect to reach the goal(s)? In the next month? by the end of the year?

The goal of growing lead generation by 50 percent could be precise, quantifiable feasible, and achievable If you don't have a date to achieve the objective, your efforts as well as your time and resources could be diverted elsewhere.

3. Find the the Ideal Customers

If a business suffers due to low social pages typically, it's due to a lack of an accurate and ideal profile of their customers. Buyer personas allow you to define and target the most relevant people in the right locations, at the appropriate moments, and with the appropriate messages.

If you know your audience's age, profession earnings, issues, interests, pains and obstacles, as well as their habits, preferences as well as their motivations and objections it's more efficient and cost-effective to reach them via social media or other channels. The more specific you can be the better conversion rates you'll get from every platform you employ to promote your company.

4. Research Competition

In the realm of advertising on social networks, studying your competition isn't just keeping you up-to-date on their activities and activities, but it also provides you with an understanding of what's working, so that you can incorporate the strategies that are successful to your own strategies. Begin by making an inventory of at least three major competitors. Find out which social media platforms they're using and then analyze their strategy for content. Take a look at their amount of followers or followers as well as their frequency of posting and the time of day. Also , pay attention to the kind of content they're sharing and the context (humorous or promotional.) and how they're responding their followers.

The most crucial thing to be focusing on is engagement. Although page administrators have the sole power to estimate the percentage of engagement on any update and you'll be able to have a better idea of what they're experiencing.

As an example, suppose you're looking at competitor's most recent 20-30 updates on Facebook. Consider the total number of engagement activities on those posts and divide that number by the total number of followers. (Engagement activity can be defined as comments, likes and shares and more.)

It is possible to use this formula on all the social media profiles (e.g. On Twitter there is a way to determine retweets as well as favorites). Remember that the calculations are meant to provide you with a broad image of what your other competitors are performing so you can assess your performance against one another.

5. Select Channels and Tactics

Many companies create accounts on each popular social media platform without determining which one will yield the highest returns. It is possible to avoid spending your time on the wrong site by using the data of your personas for buyers in order to decide which one is the most suitable for your business. If your clients or prospects say they spend 40 percent of their time online using Facebook and 20 percent on Twitter, then you'll can determine which of the principal and second social media platforms you should concentrate on.

If your clients are on the same platform it's the place you need to be - not anywhere and everywhere else. The strategies you employ for each social media channel depend on your objectives and goals in addition to the best practices for every platform. For instance, if your objective is to increase leads and your main social media platform is Facebook Some effective strategies include investing in Facebook promotions or advertising to attract more attention to the lead-generating opportunities you have.

6. Create a Content Strategy

Social media and content have mutually beneficial relationships without great content, social media is useless, while without the social network no one will be aware of your content. Utilize them in conjunction to make your content more accessible and convert potential customers.

Three main elements are essential for a successful strategy for social media content three main components: the nature of content, timing of posting, and frequency posting.

The kind of content that you post to each social media platform is based on the form and the context. Form is the way you convey that information: text and images only. hyperlinks videos, text, etc.

Context can be a good fit with your company's voice and trends on platforms. Does your content have to be entertaining or serious, extremely thorough and informative or something different?

There are numerous studies that offer an exact time frame to post your content to social networks. However, I recommend following those studies as guidelines instead of strict guidelines. Remember that your audience is individual, which is why you must experiment and determine the most effective time for you.

The frequency of your posts is just as important just as content that you post. You don't want to upset your followers or your fans are you?

The right frequency to choose is vital because it can result in more people engaging with your posts or more dislikes and unfollows. Check

Facebook Insights for the time your fans are online and are engaging with your content.

7. Allocate Budget and Resources

For budgeting for marketing on social media take a look at the strategies you've selected to meet your goals and objectives for your business. You should create a complete listing of all the equipment you'll require (e.g. the tools for social media monitoring, marketing via email, and CRM) and services that you'll outsource (e.g. video or graphic design) as well as any advertising you'll buy. On each of them, add the estimated cost for each year to provide you with an overall picture of what you're spending your money on and how it impacts the marketing budget.

Many companies establish their budget first. They decide on the best tactics to are in line with their budget. I prefer the opposite method. I first develop a plan before determining the budget that is compatible with the strategy.

If the costs of executing your strategy exceed the budget estimates Prioritize your strategies in accordance with their ROI timeframe. The strategies that have the highest ROI (e.g. advertising, social media as well as social referral) are the most important since they can generate immediate profits you can then invest in longer-term strategies (fan acquisition, high-quality content production, or longer-term involvement).

8. Assign Roles

Being aware of who's accountable for what improves efficiency and helps avoid confusion and duplicate efforts. It can be messy at first but over time, team members will be aware of their roles, and the each day tasks they're responsible for.

Once everyone has a clear understanding of the role of each person is the time to begin making plans for the process of execution. It is possible to plan either for a daily or weekly. I would not recommend making an annual plan because numerous things could be thrown up, and you might be wasting time trying to adapt to changes. Use tools like Basecamp and ActiveCollab to oversee the team, assigning tasks every member. These tools can save you lots of time and can help you keep your team organised.

The Laws of Social Media Marketing

The strategies employed by social media marketing are only effective if certain rules are adhered to and certain laws are followed that offer a the ability to lead to success with promotional campaigns. These laws serve as the base for promotional efforts of a business , to increase the effectiveness of marketing for the company, or even the branding. Utilizing the power of content as well as social media-based marketing will increase your reach and your customer base in a significant way. However, starting out without prior knowledge or experience can be a challenge.

It is essential to understand the fundamentals of social media marketing. From maximising the quality of your content to expanding your entry points to the internet following these 10 rules will allow you to create a solid foundation to benefit your customers, your business and most importantly, your bottom line.

1. "The Law of Listening

Achieving success with content marketing and social media requires more listening, not talking. Learn about your viewers' online content and participate in discussions to understand what they value most. Only then can you develop content that sparks discussions that bring value rather than merely adding to their lives.

2. Law of Focus: The Law of Focus

It's better being a master of all trades. A well-defined content marketing and social media strategy designed to build an effective brand has greater chance of the success of a broad approach which tries to cater to everyone.

3. Law of Quality Law of Quality

Quality over quantity. It's better to have 1000 online connections who are able to read, share and discuss it with your own audience than having 10,000 connections are gone after having connected with you for the first time.

4. "The Law of Patience

Content marketing and social media achievement doesn't happen in a flash. Although it's possible to see lightning in bottles, it's more likely you'll have to be committed to for the long run to see outcomes.

5. "The Law of Compounding

If you write exceptional, quality content and create an online community of high-quality followers, they'll be sharing it with their own audience through Twitter, Facebook, LinkedIn as well as their own blogs and many more.

Sharing and discussing your content can open up new ways for search engines such as Google to discover it through search results for keywords. These entry points can lead to hundreds or thousands of possible ways that people can locate you online.

6. Law of Influence Law of Influence

Take time to find the online influential people in your market that have a loyal following that are more likely to take interest in product or services as well as your business. Meet with them and build relationships with them.

If you're in their eyes as an authoritativeand interesting source of valuable information, they could publish your information to their own followers. This could place your company and you before a massive new market.

7. Law of Value Law of Value

If you are spending all your time on the Web advertising your products and services, they will not be interested. You need to add value the conversation. Concentrate less on conversions rather than creating great content and building relationships with influential people on the web. Over time, those influencers can become an effective source of word-of-mouth advertising for your company.

8. the law of acknowledgement

It's not like you would ignore those who reach out to you personally, so don't be apathetic online. Building relationships is among the most important aspects of a successful social media marketing campaign So, always be sure to acknowledge each person who is reaching out to you.

9. the Law of Accessibility

Don't post your content only to then go under the radar. Keep your content available to your viewers. This means that you must constantly publish content and take part in conversation. Online followers can be unpredictable and aren't afraid to replace you should you are absent for a period of time, whether it's a few weeks or months.

10. It is the Law of Reciprocity

It's impossible to expect other people to post your posts or speak about you if they aren't doing the same for them. Therefore, a part of your time in social networking should be centered on sharing and discussing the content posted by other people.

The benefits of Social Media Marketing

Social media has gained an image among some as being a passing interest in marketing and, consequently, unprofitable because of its rapid growth. The numbers, however, provide a different perspective. According to Hubspot 92 percent of marketers in 2014 said that using social media for marketing was essential to their company with 80% saying that their efforts helped increase the number of visitors to their sites. According to Social Media Examiner, 97 percent of marketers are taking part in social media. However, the majority of users aren't certain which social media tools are most appropriate to use.

This shows the enormous possibility for using social media to improve sales, however there is a insufficient understanding of how to make those results happen. Let's take a look at some ways that social media marketing can help your business's performance:

1. Greater Brand Recognition. Every opportunity to syndicate your content to improve your visibility is beneficial. Social media platforms are just new channels to promote your brand's voice and its content. This is crucial since it makes you accessible to new customers, as well as making your brand more recognizable and well-known for your

existing customers. For instance, a frequent Twitter user might discover your business in the very first instance after seeing it appear in an update. Another person might become more familiar with your brand following the discovery of your profile on several social networks.

2. Better brand loyalty. According to a study published in the name of Texas Tech University, brands that engage with social media platforms enjoy greater satisfaction from their customers. According to the report "Companies should make use of the opportunities social media offers in engaging with their customers. A well-thought out and transparent social media plan can be beneficial in changing consumers into loyal brand advocates." Another study conducted by Convince&Convert discovered that 53 percent of Americans who follow brands on social media are more loyal the brands they follow.

3. More Chances to Convert. Every post you post on a social media site offers customers the chance to convert. If you've built an audience, you'll be able to connect with new customers, customers who have recently visited and even old customers and will be able to communicate with them all. Every blog article or image, video, or comment you post is an opportunity for

people to respond, and each response could result in an online visit and ultimately, the conversion. Every interaction with your company results in a conversion. However, every positive interaction improves the chance of a conversion. Even if your click-through rate are low, the quantity of opportunities you can avail through social media is substantial. As I mentioned in my article "The 4 Elements of Every Action and How to Make Use of Them in the course of your Online Marketing Initiative," "opportunity" is the most important component of any strategy.

4. Increased conversion rates. Social media marketing can result in more conversion rates in a variety of distinct ways. One of the most important factor is its humanization component which is the fact that a brand are more human when they engage with social media platforms. Social media is a platform that brands can be as individuals do. This is vital because people prefer doing business with people rather than with businesses.

In addition, research has proven that social media have an 80% higher conversion rate than outbound marketing. Furthermore, having a greater number of followers on social media increases confidence and trust in your company, which is social evidence. Therefore, just building your social media following can increase the conversion rate of your current traffic.

5. Higher Brand Authority. Engaging regularly with your customers will show your trust and respect for your customers. When people want to praise or boast about the product or service they are talking about or product, they will go to social media. When they share your company name, the people who are new to your audience will be inclined to keep up with your updates. The more people are talking about your brand through social media platforms, the greater credible and trustworthy your brand's image will appear to the new audience. In addition that if you are able to connect with prominent influencers via Twitter as well as other media platforms your credibility and reach will increase dramatically.

6. More Inbound Traffic. Without social media your inbound traffic is limited to those acquainted with the brand as well as people searching for keywords that you are currently ranked for. Each social media profile you add to your profile is a different route that leads back to your site and each piece of content you share on these profiles provides an chance to attract

a new user. The more high-quality content you distribute via social media, the higher the amount of inbound traffic you'll attract which will result in more leads and greater conversions.

7. Reduced marketing costs. According to Hubspot 84% of the marketers said that just six hours of work per week could bring in more traffic. Six hours isn't an investment of a large amount for a medium as broad such as the social web. If you are able to dedicate an hour or so a day to establishing your syndication and content strategy and you can begin to see the fruits of your labor. Paid advertising on Facebook as well as Twitter is fairly inexpensive (depending on your objectives and objectives, of course). Start small, and you won't need to worry about overspending. Once you've gotten a feel about what you can expect to pay and you're able to increase the amount you budget for and increase your conversions accordingly.

8. Better Search Engine Rankings. SEO is the most effective method to get pertinent traffic coming from the search engines however the requirements to be successful change constantly. It's not enough to update your blog regularly and ensure that you have the best quality title tags as well as Meta Descriptions,

or also distribute hyperlinks that link back to your website. Google along with other major search engines could be calculating their rankings based on the presence of social media as a key factor due to the fact that brands with a strong reputation generally make use of social media. Therefore, being present on the social web may be an "brand indication" for search engines, indicating that your business is trustworthy, reliable and reliable. In other words, when you're trying to rank on a specific list of terms, having a robust social media presence is practically essential.

9. Richer Customer Experiences. Social media, at its heart is a communications channel as is phone calls and email. Every interaction you make with customers on social media provides an opportunity to show your customer service skills and enhance the relationship you have with customers. If, for instance, someone complains about your product via Twitter You are able to immediately respond to the complaint make an apology publicly and then take steps to correct the situation. If a customer is kind to you, you can be grateful and suggest other products. This is a personal gesture that lets your customers know that you appreciate them.

10. Improved customer insights. Social media can also provide you with the opportunities to gather useful information regarding the things your customers are looking for and the way they behave through social listening. For instance, you can look over user comments to determine what people's opinions are about your company directly. You can also segment your lists of content syndication by topic, and determine what types of content attract the most interest, and then create more of that kind of content. It is possible to convert from different promotions on different social media channels and finally find the ideal combination of content to earn income.

The longer you put off longer, the more you stand to lose. The use of social media for marketing executed properly, can bring increased traffic, more customers and higher conversions and it's staying.

Chapter 3: Snap Chat Marketing

The above mentioned parameters that are associated with social media marketing as well as social marketing in general have an a significant role to play in the promotion of businesses via social media channels. Every social media has its own distinct features however the function of marketing is the same. Each platform makes use of interactions as a way to create a sense of urgency to advertise its brand, product or service by employing a concise well-written, socially rich language that appeals to viewers. However, the particular media platform that Snapchat employs makes it hard to connect with other types of social media to promote marketing.

Snapchat was first introduced in 2011, and then exploded into mainstream in the year following Facebook tried but was unsuccessful in bringing it down however, brands have been slow to accept the platform. Snapchat is a text-only mobile application that lets users send a video or photo "snap" which is automatically deleted after viewing. The sender has the option of choosing the length of time that the snap is visible up to 10 seconds. After that, the message is deleted forever.

According to Snapchat's internal statistics There more than 60 percent of U.S. smartphone users aged 13-34 who are Snapchat users. If you are looking to connect with 13 to 34-year olds is your goal, Snapchat is the best social platform to invest in. 13-34-year-olds are in love with Snapchat due to three reasons:

* Perspective. Snaps allow users and their family members the opportunity to share how they view the world.

* Real-time stories. Snapchat stories are live that are updated in real time, and are only available in the span of 24 hours.

* Self-expression. By snaps, users are able to display to the world what they are at any given moment.

Though the majority of Snapchat's viewers are younger people however, there are an average of 12% of people between the ages of 35 and 54-year-olds as well as the 2% of older people can also be Snapchatters. In actuality, each day, Snapchatters get over 7 billion viewers on Snapchat. Additionally, there are over 100 million actively Snapchatters who use the app every single day.

What is it that makes Snapchat distinct in comparison to other platforms for social media is its capability to create an individual connection with the user. Contrary to other social networks which publish their posts publicly Snapchat is presented as specific to the user even though the photo itself may have been sent out to the entire population!

It allows your business the chance to create the bonds of a person. Snaps cannot be shared or distributed to other people and therefore makes the user feel special when they get a photo.

Snapchat Marketing Guidelines and Tactics

Utilizing Snapchat Snapchat app to interact to a persona of a potential buyer can be a challenge. It is important to note that Snapchat sets a limit to the length of time that the videos and pictures are available in the app. For example, a video or image will disappear after just a few seconds pass and never be seen by the person who received it. Therefore, marketers must to maximize every minute they have through the app, and this requires an amount of planning.

Understanding Your Audience

If your users are a small group of executives, it's essential to understand the nuances of Snapchat. Since its beginnings, Snapchat has been an app that promotes informal communications through the use of pictures and videos. Users snap pictures of their meals, holidays and other activities that they send to friends - they do not typically record professional behaviour.

It's crucial to look at the overall casuality of Snapchat's user interface. When your marketing department is developing a plan for Snapchat it is essential choose the language that can be utilized across all platforms. The language you choose to use should be simple to understand and your posts must convey a sense of enjoyment. Consider, for instance, using the drawing feature on Snapchat which lets you add edits to your pictures. This will help your team appear more friendly and accessible - all of which are added advantages when you try to reach out to your target customers.

If you're only beginning your journey using Snapchat make sure to research. Explore different accounts, and then follow people to get a clearer idea of their use of Snapchat.

Take it on as Ephemeral

If you are planning to utilize Snapchat as a medium to promote your business You must consider its time-limit feature as a chance to make it work, not a hindrance. Why Snapchat has caught the attention of numerous young phone users is due to the fact that the time-limit draws their attention, keeps it and leaves the users in a state of laughter, squirting their heads or in a state of silence. Non-profits that use this platform have to follow the same pattern in their marketing campaigns.

What I find fascinating about self-destructing content is the way it is connected to the issues that have been raised about the nature of creating content on the internet. It has given users with the opportunity to people like me to post free of charge, giving readers with information previously unobtainable however, this has brought new problems.

One of these are managing the information. The appeal of Snapchat or a similar platform Snapchat is the fact that it's temporary, meaning that we don't need to go through a lot of messages.

The focus should be on building relationships

A smaller, more engaged audience is more crucial for non-profit organizations than reaching a huge unengaged audience.

It's not about how many people you follow, but how many people care. It's not the width, but its depth. It's not the number of impressions you'll get, it's how involved they are in your cause.

Snapchat is an instant individual experience that results in high engagement. It allows nonprofits to strengthen relationships with their patrons due to the apparent intimacy of Snapchat.

Applying this idea to non-profit organisations, sending donation specific Snaps can increase the involvement of donors with the projects they support as they observe the impact that their contributions make on the project, or share behind-the-scenes images of the programs you're providing and the work you are doing. Giving this kind of intimate accessibility will make donors feel more connected to your cause.

Accepting the Time Limit

Although some might consider the self-destructing nature Snapchat as a problem marketing professionals can really make an impact using this feature of the application. In particular, Technorati states that this allows you to provide teasers to your users on Snapchat. Since photos and videos last only short periods of time it is possible to use Snapchat to provide people with the chance to preview the forthcoming product or service which your company might offer.

Additionally, you can utilize Snapchat to organize contests. For example, you could invite your users to send photos of themselves using your product, and then give a prize to users who participate. The key to getting the most benefit from Snapchat is to make sure that you're constantly looking for ways to interact the customers you serve. This will keep them returning to your site which gives you more chances to develop your marketing plan.

Start Moving by watching a video

Snapchat isn't only about self-destructing pictures Videos are an essential aspect of the site too. While they do disappear after they've been seen and viewed by marketers, they can be used to contact users who are curious to get a glimpse into their office culture, production of products and all the rest.

Marketing departments can utilize video to offer more useful information to their customers. Though they say a photo is worth the words it can effectively communicate the message you're trying communicate to your followers by using videos. Additionally is that you don't have to be a professional in order to create a buzz. Keep in mind that Snapchat is about being informal and relatable.

Reflecting Your Personality

In the same way as all digital media Snapchat provides you with a chance to show the real motives and goals of your business, regardless of whether that's providing services or a useful product. The content you upload to Snapchat should give users an idea of the company and what you have to provide. It is important to add personality to your images and videos in order to allow people to connect to your brand at the "human-like" level. This is this is a topic I addressed in my piece, "Why It's Important to make your brand more human Brand through Social Media."

Snapchat is, just like Twitter, Facebook, and Google+ before it, will likely add additional features as it develops. One of the latest features was the introduction of Snapchat Stories, a feature that allows brands to create and connect a story throughout the course of the day. Stories can be viewed many times before the 24-hour hours have expired and after that they are deleted. Clips are removed piece-by- each as they hit the end of the day and new ones are added at the conclusion of the story.

The capacity for Snapchat Stories to construct an entire day-long story allows for innovative applications of Snapchat by companies. Brands are now able to create an interactive and connected story for their users, rather than relying on single-shot snaps. Like Vine created flipbook-style videos for companies; Snapchat offers a platform for content that creates a unified story that isn't impacted by other accounts, and permits the creation of a narrative constructed.

This is a great way to demonstrate how things are progressing and changing during the course of a 24-hour period. Particularly for organizations that focus on emergency relief or rehabilitation the idea of a 24-hour story telling period could be a huge impact. Make use of Snapchat to showcase more than just content but also to show what's happening behind the behind the scenes. Invite other employees in your business to join your Snapchat efforts in order to give it some spice. As time passes, you'll be able to notice the difference in the speed with which your followers grow.

Snapchat at A Glance

If you're not sure whether it's worth making use of Snapchat to market your business take a look at these numbers. There are about 26 million

Snapchat users in U.S., and about 400 million snaps are shared every day. If you're not making use of Snapchat in your strategy for marketing it could mean you're not utilizing the chance to reach out to a variety of people that are part of your ideal customer base. There's more to connecting with your audience than simply installing the application.

If you take these information into consideration, you'll be able to be sure you're unlocking every bit of the potential that is Snapchat.

Tips to Make the Most of Snapchat

1. Stage an Influencer Uncover

The global fast-food company McDonald's (username: McDonalds) isn't only about a famous clown who sells toys along with an entrée. Professional athletes such as LeBron James provided users with an insider's view into the launch of the brand bacon sandwich. Even though McDonald's did not release the outcomes of the promotion however, it was successful enough to be able to carry on. The campaign was then pushed out onto Twitter which users were prompted to follow McDonald's back. So far, McDonald's has over 3 million Twitter followers.

Takeaway: You can use the same concept to Snapchat to offer your customers an insight into what goes in the background of your business. Even even if your marketing budget is just a tiny small fraction of the amount McDonald's is, customers want to feel like they have a sense of the history about your company.

2. Support for an Account Takeover

The renowned young women's clothing seller Wet Seal (username: wetseal) began an Snapchat campaign that was swiftly taken over an Snapchatter known as MsMeghanMakeup.

Meghan has more than 300,000 followers, and her impact was immediately felt as a halo effect on The campaign for Wet Seal. The boost boosted the company to 9,000 social media followers in two weeks, and more than 250,000 views on this festive "story." Wet Seal won the sixth annual Shorty Awards, which honors the top social media stars.

In order to get your message heard it is possible to allow a prominent Snapchat user control your account. It's possible that you don't have connections to 300K+ followers however, even local authorities that have hundreds or thousands of followers could increase you Snapchat reach.

3. Share Promo Codes

16 Handles, the frozen yogurt chain (username"love16handles") made use of Snapchat's instant picture feature to build a following and spread the word about their frozen treats. They were one of the first brands to make use of Snapchat to promote coupons.

The company's yogurt brand gained new customers by advertising specific locations and times at the stores as well as when customers snapped pictures of themselves or companions enjoying the 16 Handles Yogurt, they immediately were given a coupon that was between 16 percent and 100 percent off. The catch was that they only needed 10 seconds to present the coupon to the cashier.

The lesson to take away is that you can get your followers to join Snapchat with exclusive coupons and other special promotions. Have fun, and your brand's popularity will surely grow!

4. Provide VIP Access

It used to take a few weeks for images taken at New York Fashion Week to be distributed from the photographers to magazines and then on to newsstands, customers. With Snapchat the users can see the fashions change in a flash.

Lucky Magazine's editor in chief and fashion label Refinery 29, and many others posted photos of models walking down the catwalk, allowing them show images from the legendary fashion show to the public in ways they've never thought of before.

The lesson to take away is that you can use Snapchat to provide your followers with the chance to see inside your promotions and events that will likely never get a opportunity to experience in person. It's an enjoyable, easy way to give fresh life to your events.

5. Highlight Your Followers

Food ordering on the web and mobile company GrubHub (username: Grubhub) has launched their debut Snapchat advertising campaign back in the year 2013 winning the 7th annual Shorty Awards. They showcased their own content on a weekly basis, along with stories that were compiled from user-generated content as well as giveaways and promotions.

The results also showed the growth of 20% in followers following the announcement of the Snapchat giveaway. The campaign was among several factors that led to the company's Wall Street debut in a public offering.

Be careful not to allow the content you share on your Snapchat feed become self-serving. Create your feed to be about your followers, provide them with something of value and involve them in the creation of content.

6. Demo Your Product

Amazon, the world's largest retail site, Amazon (username the company is: Amazon) utilized Snapchat to give voice and personality to Alexa Amazon's woman-voiced Echo speaker. Through a clever use of the social network, Amazon employed Snapchat to clarify the product that was confusing people when it was first introduced in the first place, and also to advertise Echo.

Through its campaign, Amazon got 6,100 mentions only four hours. It proved that Echo was on the right track to be a success.

In the event that your brand introduces new products or technology that aren't yet available, you can use Snapchat as a reference for new customers. It's a smart method to utilize

Snapchat to showcase new products and interact with prospective customers.

7. Join forces with Influencers

Sour Patch Kids (username: SourpatchSnaps) is a huge hit in the Snapchat group and is the target market for the brand. Mondelez the company that owns the brand, partnered with popular social media user Logan Paul to produce content for chats.

In the span of 5 days Paul took pictures of childish tricks that were played on innocents and pranks were dubbed "sweet" or "sour" to draw attention to the flavors of the brand. The brand urged fans to post their photos and share each story. The campaign brought Sour Patch Kids 120,000 new Snapchat followers.

Learn from this: Work with an influencer who's follower has a similar base to that of yours and post photos that match the image of your brand. For Sour Patch Kids, pranks and general humour work well both in terms of creating a brand identity as well as in enthralling the followers of the brand. The results could be different for you.

8. Speak to relevant issues

Historically, the soap brand Dove (username Dove) was a favorite among females over the age of 40 until they began reaching the younger females via Snapchat. Over the course that lasted two hours thirty women sat down with psychologists , as well as other brand ambassadors via Snapchat to discuss ideas and thoughts on self-esteem issues as part of a campaign designed to increase confidence in young women's self-image.

The results of the snaps earned Dove 75 conversations and 130,000 views. This led Dove to state that they'll continue to track the engagement as well as reaching (conversations) as an element of their campaign measures going forward.

The lesson: When you're on Snapchat do not feel shy about being authentic. Being authentic is crucial in this highly-social platform.

9. Offer Exclusive Previews

Business Insider reported that Acura (username: Acura_insider) made use of Snapchat to generate excitement for its racecar-inspired NSX. Acura gave 100 followers a special glimpse of the NSX's new model. The first 100 followers received this video of the fast luxurious car.

Acura was selected as a finalist for the 6th annual Shorty Awards after successfully integrating Snapchat into its advertising campaign. The campaign generated lots of attention for Acura that the company then repurposed to Instagram, Vine, and Twitter.

Learn how to offer a reward to your most loyal customers and followers also. Offer exclusive information to only a small number of people. It's possible to do this regardless of whether you're an international auto manufacturer or locally-based "mom and pop" retailer.

10. Promote Events

iHeartRadio (username:"iheartradio") utilized Snapchat to record and share the iHeartRadio Music Festival. For the duration of two days, the organization racked up an impressive 340 million impressions through the efforts of enthusiastic festival goers who shared their experience. The festival became a viral hit on Snapchat.

The ephemeral nature of Snapchat makes it the perfect choice to promote events that are limited in time. Include it in your next event to offer your fans an insider's view.

Best Marketing Brands for Snapchat Snapchat

Companies from all industries and across a variety of demographics such as Sour Patch Kids to General Electric and HubSpot are using Snapchat to interact with their followers and customers with a low-cost method yet extremely personal and entertaining. The posts they make in Snapchat isn't polished. It's messy and sloppy and enjoyable. It's true that Snapchat is about letting your brand's personal style shine through and connecting to your audience in a completely human way.

1. Sour Patch Kids

The first users of Snapchat were teenagers. This provided the snack manufacturer, Modelez, an incentive to join Snapchat to promote its Sour Patch Kids candy brand.

In 2014 one of the company's main objectives was to raise the brand's popularity among their primary segment: the candy-loving teens of the United States. As teens were spending ever-increasing amounts of time on Snapchat and other social media platforms, they decided to create entertaining content that users could use to share their experiences with their friends.

To launch the promotional campaign "Real-Life Sour Patch Kids" the brand collaborated to Logan Paul, a social media influencer and comedian who recorded for five days the pranks that took place around New York City via Snapchat. It was a play on the tagline of the brand, "First they're sour, then they're sweet" when the pranks varied from "sweet" at the start during the course of five days and then more "sour" jokes throughout the course of the week. Every month fresh Stories were released that showed"Real Sour Patch Kids "Real Sour Patch Kids" pretending to be normal teens.

2. Everlane

The retailer Everlane was also a early Snapchat user however, with a more bold approach to the new social media platform. In November of 2015 they published this statement the official post on their website: "We're here to make an unorthodox claim. Snapchat will soon be the official social media channel for Everlane. In the last month, we've been experimenting with small batches of the service and we're in love."

Why did they like the site so in such a way? It was because they saw it as the best way to show their unique approach to transparency than other social media platforms like Facebook.

"Facebook is a platform to keep our community updated and having one-on-one discussions," read the post. "But Snapchat is completely different. Snapchat lets us to experiment with transparency in a totally different method. No fancy cameras. No editing. Raw, live footage. It's stunning, and it's the perfect platform for the current generation."

A year and a half later, they've not changed their minds. The people at Everlane utilize Snapchat as access to their e-commerce company, events along with their life. They utilize their Snapchat Story feature to create stories about tours of their premises as well as interviewing customers in their brick-and-mortar stores and showing off new products. On #TransparencyTuesday, for example, they use Snapchat to record a walkthrough of their business or factories.

3. General Electric

Did you think the possibility that General Electric, a multinational conglomerate is a prominent and efficient online presence Snapchat?

They've done an amazing job making use of their platform to display their geeky side and stimulate interest in sciencean approach they've successfully used on other social media sites such as Instagram as well as YouTube.

One of the most effective methods they utilize the platform is to create an ongoing series where they respond to questions from users by explaining the scientific concept in a simple and enjoyable manner. For instance, they have recently published some of the findings from their Emoji Science curriculumthat they developed in conjunction and with National Science Foundation.

Alongside sharing their findings from the field of emojis and encouraging their Snapchat followers to communicate direct with them. "Just include the word "generalelectric" on Snapchat and contact us with an emoticon and we'll give you some research," they wrote on their Tumblr.

Global director of innovation for GE Sam Olstein said about Snapchat, "The disappearing nature of Snapchat's content is a great incentive to use it again and gives us the opportunity to celebrate innovation with an increasing number of young users."

4. Gatorade

Gatorade does not have a Snapchat account that's its own, but due to their incredible sponsored lens Snapchat during the Super Bowl this year, we believe they merit an inclusion in this top 10 list. (Note that a Snapchat lens is basically an innovative filter to use with your selfies. You can see what happens when you see your friends post Snapchats that show them puking rainbows.)

This is what they did If the football team is victorious and wins, the players dump the sports drink that's inside the cooler of the team on the head of their coach. At this year's Super Bowl football game in 2016, the people at PepsiCo's owned Gatorade created a unique Super Bowl Snapchat lens that let anyone take an Gatorade bath, too.

In order to create the ad Gatorade's folks Gatorade joined forces with Snapchat to buy the lens for sponsorship, which is priced at around $450,000 for a sponsored lens during normal times and $750,000 on "peak days" such as holidays and Super Bowl. Super Bowl.

Then, they brought in pro tennis star Serena Williams -- whom Gatorade is a sponsor of. The commercial showed Williams being practically "dumped upon" in a cooler filled with orange Gatorade due to the lens. The company tweeted an GIF that was uploaded to Snapchat to keep the momentum moving. And at the time the event was over the lens was been seen over 100 million times.

5. Warby Parker

Warby Parker, Snapchat is used for a variety of purposes. Warby Parker, Snapchat is utilized for a range of subjects: from showcasing the products ("Today on Snapchat we're trying to make our most-loved Crystal frames in just 15 minutes") to offering users the chance to speak with the co-founder of the company, Neil Blumenthal ("Our co-founder Neil Blumenthal is in the private room today. Watch to Snapchat to hear him answer your questions! ").

They've got a variety of Snapchat series that include a brand new one dubbed "Desk job." In a most recent Snapchat Story, they featured one of their creative directors on his top five desk necessities. When an Snapchat Story is up, they promote it through Twitter, Instagram, and LinkedIn. (I saw that they didn't advertise their stories on Facebook this is an advantage: On Facebook it's crucial to choose what content you post and to be focused on the quality, rather than the quantity of content.)

6. GrubHub

GrubHub is as well as an early Snapchat user is putting out news on a weekly basis since the end of 2013. However, they use Snapchat in a different way than most of the people included on this list. Instead of producing content that is only one-way, GrubHub focuses on building an active and engaged community by posting Snapchat messages that need to be answered with coupons that are exclusive contests, giveaways and contests and coupons for promotions.

They were among the only brands to engage with virtually every Snapchat message received by their users, each all week. At the time of the 2014 end, GrubHub had earned the most impressive Snapchat scores of any company (53,668 at the at the time). Their commitment to engage led to them being a finalist for the Shorty Awards.

7. New York Times

The editors, writers, and others working at The New York Times use Snapchat in a different wayoccasionally, they poke fun at their ignorance of the app, and other times making use of it as a storytelling platform (and afterwards, reviewing it in writing later).

There was a Snapchat Story which was part of an investigation of what constitutes an objectively great Snapchat Story and resulted in this article written by Talya Minsberg. In the piece, she asked journalists from The Times to participate in an online challenge to make an objectively excellent Snapchat Story.

What makes an objectively good Snapchat Story? Minsberg declares it's difficult for anyone to pinpoint, yet she does say "the top Snapchat stories are generally those that tell a story with a unique, personal manner that draws in and captivates the viewers."

Another significant takeaway from her article is this: "Even Snapchat stories must be held to the same standards of quality as anything other content that is published in The Times. There are more doodles, emojis and doodles in the Snapchat story than what you read printed in the paper!"

8. DJ Khaled

DJ Khaled might not seem like the most popular company, but he's completely changed the way celebrities are seen on Snapchat and there's a lot that brands can learn from DJ Khaled. In March of 2016 and less than an entire year since DJ Khaled had even heard of Snapchat It was revealed the fact that DJ Khaled's Snapchats were drawing three million to four million users every single day.

What is his secret? The first thing is that his way of making videos is efficient. He enjoys combining regular daily tasks -- such as applying deodorant and watering the flowers -- along with humorous remarks and short quips.

There are some mantras which he repeats, such as "another one" and "bless up," which he's parlayed into some expensive products. He also enjoys sharing "keys to wisdom" and even purchased his own geofilter during an excursion in Las Vegas for New Year's Eve (which is something anyone can do, by way).

A combination of behindstage pass-style topics, hilarious one-liners and a fun use of emojis make Khaled's Instagram account extremely accessible and easy to follow.

9. Domino's Pizza UK

The team of Dominos Pizza have never been scared to explore the latest social channels. They were the first company to make use of Tinder in conjunction with a campaign in 2015. Valentine's Day campaign, and their "Tweet to Eat" campaign allowed customers to order pizza through Twitter by sending an emoji representing pizza.

In terms of their global reach their social media teams across the globe have embraced Snapchat at various times. For instance, Dominos Australia started using Snapchat in

2013, and was able to send their Snapchat Stories that aligned with initiatives they were already running through social media.

It's true that the U.K. team at Dominos Pizza was not on Snapchat until January 2016 however they began with a really cool experiment that resulted in an increase in orders. On the 20th of January in 2016, they repurposed the story of their Snapchat Story into a short movie called "Dough from Door."

This film follows the story of an Dominos delivery truck driver, who encounters some hurdles on his way to deliver pizza to a customerand even being attacked by aliens. According to the Drum the film also displayed a series of random letters through the film that equate to a discount coupon they could use later on the internet.

Dominos' employees Dominos discovered that the budget-friendly project has led to an increase in the number of orders. "The film drove more orders than we anticipated, even though it wasn't a huge driving factor for us." Nick Dutch, Dominos chief of digital strategy said to Business Insider.

Because Snapchat does not offer anything in terms of analytics (unless you're making use of

Snapchat to promote your business) the only way that the Dutch team could explain the rise in sales to Snapchat was due to the discount code that was unique to SnapchatKeep this in mind when making Stories that you've created your own.

10. HubSpot

Although there are lots of B2C companies that are doing great things using Snapchat however, there are smaller B2B businesses which have managed to build an audience. This is a challenge that they decided to tackle at HubSpot and that's why they created the HubSpot Snapchat channel back in the month of March of 2016.

To ensure that our Snapchat channel useful They use it to function as a marketing as well as an avenue for recruiting -- a platform to showcase their the unique culture and perks of their employees amazing employees, as well as the idea of inbound.

In the realm of marketing they are known for giving their followers an insight into the business and show off their culture. Their goal is to make the content educational interesting, entertaining, and fun that are the most well-known goals of Marketing's team.

For instance in the event that BuzzFeed News Editor Rachel Zarrell was invited to HubSpot just a few weeks ago to discuss the importance of viral media, HubSpot showed some of her talks -and what the employees thought of it following the event -on Snapchat.

In terms of culture They want to present HubSpot as a place to visit -hoping to encourage users to explore other online offerings like their website, blog as well as their careers page and the list goes on. The most important thing for us is employing a natural voice that is appropriate for Snapchat's Snapchat world, not one that is snooty or professional.

11. The Kardashians

The Kardashians gained fame through their reality show of the same name," Keeping up with Kardashians". With a continuous ascendance to power, most notably by the questionable ways that Kim Kardashian uses, now , the Kardashians are regarded as the reigning queen of social media use. They are among the most followed individuals using Snapchat and have employed the platform to promote their products for commercial use. They can be selling makeup kits and mobile games, emojis, designer clothing or shoes.

They've perfected the art that is Social Media Marketing, and experts have discovered that their sales marketing could solely be due to the effect due to the use of Snapchat Marketing.

From promotions, exhibitions to previews of the background they are able to showcase their products. through Kim advertising her Emoji jewelry and stickers to Kylie showing off the distinctive shades of her lipstick line , and Kendall giving sneak peeks to her photography shoots. Kim has also utilized her platform to showcase the husband's Yeezy Fashion line, concert tickets, and music labels. Anyone who wants to promote their product should take a look at the Social Media activity.

Chapter 4: The Importance Of The Social Media Marketing

Before we go through Snapchat in greater detail Let's look at the significance of marketing via social media in general for businesses, and then remember why it's an important channel for marketing.

In the present, it ought to not be any doubts in everyone's mind that, given the rise of internet technology and smartphones, marketing online is going to be essential to businesses' success. It's certainly possible to assert that a brand that is not active on social media could be seen as insignificant. In reality, it doesn't matter how big or successful you are social media marketing should be an integral element of your marketing plan.

Social media platforms such as Snapchat can help you connect with your clients and the wider market, which , in turn boost the awareness of your brand which will in turn lead to higher sales and conversions.

The number of users using social media worldwide is massive - well over 3 billion users are engaging with social media each day! This is your market potential.

To highlight the significance of social media to businesses 72% of users between the ages of 25 and 34 years look at the feedback and reviews about products and services via social media prior to making a purchase.

Social media platforms can allow customers to interact with you more easily and more efficient since companies can establish a customer base and interact with them by providing good-quality content. Social media have made the two sides of the sale chain accessible - customers are able to effortlessly connect with you, and the other way around.

Below are some of the most important five reasons why social media is crucial to business:

Below are the most important reasons that every business should have an online presence. Snapchat offers the features and an established track record of helping businesses make the most of these advantages.

1. Enhancing brand awareness and visibility

It is the most effective platform to enhance your brand's exposure due to the capacity to reach an enormous audience quickly and within a brief amount of duration. Social media sites such as Snapchat can increase the number of possibilities for you to share content that can be then is shared with your fans. The only thing you need to do is determine the goals of your marketing and then create an actionable strategy for social media to achieve your goals.

Through social media, you provide your customers and the public a chance to locate your company more easily since it is likely to appear in different search results, while also increasing the visibility about your company. When you have gained your followers on social media, leverage the followers you have to help spread awareness about your brand, and then continue to expand to increase the number of people who follow you and becoming aware of your business. There's no limit to your reach.

2. Communication of Business Expertise and Values

Customers are becoming more selective about what brands they choose to associate with. They are turning to social media for their due diligence and find out more about the brands they like. Mobile devices and an increased internet have transformed social media into the most popular choice for customers to conduct quick searches to find information about companies.

With a current and robust profile You can establish credibility and position your business in a positive way to anyone who is searching for you online. Inform readers about your product or services, as well as outline your experience and your niche. When you make information available about your business create trust, to ensure that future customers feel confident in dealing with your company.

3. Authenticity of the message

Social media allows you to be more genuine and personal by sharing your story instead of traditional tailored messages on websites. Provide viewers with the authentic feel of your company by using platforms like Snapchat that show exclusive behind-the scenes videos of your company's operations. Participate in conversations with followers and respond to questions and feedback faster. Be aware the fact that using social media can be a casual medium and you don't need an official letterhead, but only your real-time self.

4. Customer Engagement

There are many functions on social media that companies could use to increase customer engagement. Utilizing these features, in mixed is a great method to keep your fans and customers active. Provide information about your company as well as reply to comments and have Q&A discussions. Utilize all tools available to keep your followers engaged. Be sure to post new content frequently to keep your followers interested.

Another way to make the most of social networks is making use of user-generated content. When you comment on posts posted by users and customers you will increase their attention to your brand and will also share your content increasing your exposure to potential customers.

5. Customer Support

The accessibility to communication and interaction through social media has reduced the distance between businesses as well as their clients. Instead of sending emails or calling phones, consumers are now able to get their questions answered much faster via social media. Be a responsive and caring brand by providing quick assistance to customers via social media.

6. Marketing with a budget

Social media is economical compared to traditional methods of marketing and is the best medium for marketing and advertising for small businesses or those that don't have a large amount of money for advertising and marketing.

Marketing via social media is generally free , unless you choose paid advertising or other marketing tools that are paid for within social media, which aren't so expensive as other kinds of marketing. You can also create targeted marketing in order to make sure that your content is seen by the segment of the market you wish to reach.

7. To have an advantage over Your Competitors

There's hardly any company that isn't on social media these days. Therefore should you find out what your competition is it is essential to be taking part in the same. The only way to gain an advantage over your competition is to follow their strategies for marketing on social media. Find out how they interact with their clients and what they are talking about. If you do this you'll get an advantage over your competition by gaining more information to increase conversions and sales.

8. Perfect for targeted marketing

Social media is the ideal medium for marketing that is targeted because it offers facilities and infrastructure that allow for making use of targeted Ads that are efficient and tested for brand promotion and creating leads.

Social media marketing permits you to plan your marketing to target particular segments or demographics that increase your chance of conversions. You can target your audience based on age, location, gender, for instance. In addition, you'll be equipped with the tools needed to evaluate and monitor your performance to make the needed adjustments to allow you to boost your sales.

9. Access to relevant influencers

Utilizing influencers in social media marketing is among the most efficient methods for gaining increasing brand recognition, and also for gaining the number of followers. The influencers are active using social media, so should you be making use of them, you've been where they are.

If you are active on social media, you'll be able identify the ideal influencer to promote your brand and one that's suitable for your products or services. Engaging with influencers can positively affect your messages and improve your brand's image.

These individuals will typically have a large number of followers that they will be sharing your content with, and will share your content to their circle and thus spread your message to the masses faster and more effectively than other channel.

10. More Content Sharing Speed and More Online Traffic

The previous paragraph has highlighted how fast you can send your message to so many people who use social media. The more people who read your message, they will be referred to your website , where you'll experience an increase in traffic to your website which means better chances of sales and conversion for your company. When you post your message via social media, you'll witness a significant increase in internet traffic on all of your social media channels.

11. Professional Networking as well as Relationships Building

Utilize social media for business-to-business networking as well as to build relationships with your clients. When you share content on the internet, you'll get feedback and comments that you can utilize to engage with your audience to promote your product and turn potential customers. In essence, you should make use of social media for customer service and support . respond quickly, and updates to content fresh and frequent.

12. Enhances Your SEO (Search Engine Optimization) Rankings

A presence on social media assist by attracting more users to your site as well as other websites and other platforms, but the more visits and searches to your website the higher your SEO rank will be. Shareable content is extremely beneficial for SEO ranking improvement sharing content can increase the amount of backlinks for your pages and content on the web, and improves your possibility of having backlinks that are of high quality.

Social Media Trends to Include in your Marketing Strategy for 2019 and Beyond

As it has been stated is a crucial market for marketers and consumers are seeking more features and tools that improve their experience on social media.

In this regard, social media platforms are always searching for new tools and features to make users' experience more enjoyable, to make them more engaged in the process, more interactive and also to assist them in helping to create more content.

The success of Snapchat as well as other online platforms requires a mastery of how to provide customized experiences and content to people who use them. Companies that can find the ideal balance between authentic messages and marketing will prosper in the future, and to ensure this happens, brands have to stay on top of new trends in order to swiftly incorporate them to improve engagement with their customers.

Here are a few most important trends for the future that you must make the most of to ensure Snapchat marketing to be successful:

1. In-the-Moment Content is the Future of Online Marketing

Instead of highly-produced content, what the users of social media are looking for is content that's in-the-moment, which is something that Snapchat is the leading platform in. If you're looking for an easy definition of what is in-the-moment consider ephemeral content that requires you to comprehend your audience, be humorous, and produce new content.

Stories will become the primary device for engaging and enticing users moving forward. In reality Stories will likely be the primary method to share content via social media, particularly for companies. If you've not been making use of Stories now, it's time to understand how to utilize them and make use of them.

With the increasing use and popularity on mobile phones, shorter-lived content is expected to be the most popular especially by the younger generation. They want content that is authentic and has a personal touches - not the usual standard sales pitch.

Your content on the internet must be focused more on the individual user and make it more easy to connect with the person who is reading your content. Engage your Snapchat viewers in the background and share other exclusive content that strikes an emotional chord with them and make them follow your account. Marketing by talking with them about the everyday operations of your business They want to feel associated with the brand, not just to feel connected.

2. AI-Driven User Experience

The future will bring more artificial intelligence experience for users throughout all the social platforms. Already, with Chatbots, AI is enhancing the user experience on social media by personalizing user experiences. Numerous businesses have not yet utilized this technology and should as long as they are operating within the lawful framework for privacy.

Expect AI personalization to gain more popularity through online customer service. Artificial Intelligence tools, like Drift are currently frequently used on numerous websites, and you'll be seeing more appearing. It is expected that in two years, all interactions with customers on the internet could be AI driven.

The younger generation is taking the lead in the adoption of AI customer experience tools such as Chatbots This trend is likely to only increase. According to a report from Huffington Post, say that 60% of millennials would prefer Chatbots. AI can aid in better user-generated content It is also easy to monitor user habits and preferences using AI and produce personalized messages based on individual information.

3. Social Media Ads

In 2018 there was an increase in the use of social media. The platform is being utilized more than at any time before. Social media advertising, with features such as Snap ads, are going to become the main focus of marketers moving into the future. In the realm of advertising the brands need to be innovative and strategic as it is becoming more competitive and costly.

Because a large number of companies are in a race for attention, boring plain messages will not be enough. Utilize engaging and engaging content that has striking images to get more clicks and higher conversion rates. Instagram is a pioneer in this space and has been running Stories Ads since 2017, and since then have enabled businesses to utilize multiple photos or videos.

4. Vertical Videos and Social Media TV

With Snapchat's 5-minute TV shows, making use of their groundbreaking vertical videos, and the Instagram introduction of IGTV You can discern the direction that social media is taking. Social TV is among the upcoming big trends on social media that businesses will be able to use to promote their products.

Social media TV is expected to dramatically alter the way the content is presented in the future. A study conducted by Statista found that more than 50% of all digital content are seen with a horizontal format when viewed on phones.

5. Omni-Channel Marketing

Omni-channel marketing is the newest form of multichannel marketing. With the myriad of marketing channels accessible both offline and online it is the latest way for both marketers and businesses to approach marketing. It is an effective sales strategy that can include all channels of marketing in a manner that the message is combined, however the content is exclusive to the channel in order to ensure effectiveness.

Omni-channeling is essential as every marketer in this digital age needs to be aware that customers may be in one channel , then move to another, thereby enhancing the an experience for customers across all channels, so that it is seamless and integrated.

The traditional marketing strategy of the past century was the traditional method of marketing. you made a print radio, TV or an outdoor ad and then hoped to get it to the people you wanted to reach. Marketing was about creativity and reached and effectiveness was measured in a two-way relationship between the customer and brand was practically absent. The way of marketing is been completely flipped due to social media and has led to Omnian integral part of the new strategy.

Digital marketing that is multi-channel can be the most efficient method of attracting, engaging in communication with, getting feedback from tracking, and re-contacting users across a array of digital channels like the internet and social media, email and search engines, etc. On various deviceslike laptops, desktop computers tablet, smartphones and desktop computers and even offline one-on-one.

Omni-channel marketing enables you to reach, engage and reconnect with your prospect to guide and push them to a CTA (Call to Action) as they move through the consideration-to-purchase process, across the multiple devices they use.

1. The growth in Augmented Reality (AR)

Snapchat has recently pushed for the application of augmented reality and is among the top social media platforms when it comes to this area. Users are sharing more than 250 million AR Snaps every day, and Snapchat states that 7 of 10 users on the platform utilize AR every month.

AR is a fascinating new avenue for brands who want to reach the Snapchat users with original and original content. Adidas is currently testing

AR to sell sneakers. Essentially, buyers don't have to put on the shoes at a retail store prior to purchasing. In AR you are able to put on Adidas shoes and then buy them by clicking the Buy button.

Additionally, Snapchat has introduced Snap spectacles to improve the experience. This is one of the latest trends that make Snapchat so appealing for the younger generation.

6. The digital marketing "Holy Trinity" - Content & Search, Email and Social Media

The fundamentals of digital marketing, such as creating multi-device-friendly web content including SEM and SEO (Google) and email databases with marketing features, as well as presence on social media (Facebook and LinkedIn and LinkedIn, etc.) remain the primary tenets in digital marketing. Make sure you are familiar with these concepts prior to attempting to expand into new areas. Although email marketing has been automated with the help of technology but content marketing, social and search remain extremely complicated and labor-intensive. Certain companies have entire teams of experts within their own departments in these fields. Others contract out to these specialists.

Social media marketing has increased in importance and influence due to the fact that the market of millennials increases. These basic digital techniques are a must for marketing your business online. You will need adequate budgets, resources, and resources to implement effectively. Next "big factor" to include in this mix is according to us the data analytics software and other services.

It is evident the importance of social media. crucial in marketing and should be incorporated by companies into their marketing strategies. A well-thought out online marketing strategy should take advantage of the numerous benefits of social media that result in more traffic to your social media sites as well as your website, a better search engine optimization (SEO) rating and performance as well as an increase in the brand's recognition and customer loyalty in addition to other advantages which have been previously discussed.

In the next section we'll explore how Snapchat functions, as well as the features that make it work to promote marketing.

Chapter 5: What Is Snap Chat? Snap Chat Functions: The Most Effective Features For Marketing

Snapchat is a unique platform with different characteristics and functions that make it distinctive. We'll go over the features and delving more into the capabilities.

Before we go over these, let's take a look at the language used in the app, as you might have seen certain terms in the earlier chapter that you might not be familiar with. Maybe you've encountered them before, but aren't sure what they mean.

Here are some functions and features, as well as their definitions:

* Snap It is a photograph or video you can send through the app. Video snaps can run up to 10 seconds. You can snap the Snap and share your Snap on Snapchat to one or a group of friends. The Snap is deleted when all of the users have seen it, unless you upload the Snap to your Story that lasts up to 24 hours. If the Snap has not been opened, the person who received it is given 30 days to open it.

* Snapcode * Snapcode: This is a specific code that is similar like a QR Code smartphones can scan. It lets people follow you by simply using

their smartphone camera to scan your code and scanning it once it's open in your account. Each Snapchat user automatically gets an unique Snapcode that they can use to gain access to features and content on the platform as well as to join friends. It is also possible to generate more Snapcodes to connect to other websites.

The feature emphasizes the streak of the course of a Snap communication. Snapping with someone each day for 3 days for a period of 24 hours days is considered to be a Snapstreak and is highlighted with a flame Emoji beside the person you're in the Snapstreak with. The name of the friend and the days of the streak are noted in the chat, but regular interactions aren't considered Snapstreaks.

* Snapchat Lens lenses are used to add animations or special effects to videos or photos and unlike filters utilized following the taking of an Snap lens can be utilized during the process of taking the Snap.

* Story The Snapchat Story refers to a picture that you post publically and accessible to everyone users of the Snapchat friends. You can add pictures to your Story over an entire 24 hours period, and be shared with people following you.

Stories can be made custom and it allows groups to create Stories with each other. Custom Stories allow you to create the appearance of a Group Story - specific people can contribute Snaps or create a Geo-fenced Story. By using this feature, you can allow your friends and their friends to upload Snaps within the Story as well as Snaps from a particular location when you create Geo-fenced Story.

* Friends Snapchat followers are the ones who are following you on Snapchat as well as those who have added them on their Snapchat. They can follow you , without having to follow them in return and are in a position to see the photos you share on the public.

* Filters: They can alter how the photo or video appears. It's a fun method to add an overlay or other features to your Snaps. There is much with the filters. You can add additional details to your photos to make them more relevant or alter them so that they appear interesting and unique for viewers. You can alter filters depending on specific events, the location or timing of the day.

* Geofilter: These are referred to the filters which are exclusive to the current location or particular location. It is activated after you have turned on your location setting within

Snapchat. This feature is ideal to build brand awareness and showing off occasions.

These are just a few of the phrases and terms you'll see on Snapchat when you are doing your marketing. After you've become well-versed in the functions and common terms We can now look at how Snapchat actually functions.

How to navigate Snapchat

Snapchat will open to the camera's display in contrast to others social networks that are open to an update feed. Or a timeline. You can navigate the app by sliding left or right on the camera's screen.

Set up an Snapchat Account

Download the app

To start it is necessary to navigate to your Google Play Store for Android or the App Store for iOS and download the application. After that, you must sign up and set up your account. Follow the steps to sign-up and create your account.

Create an account

Choose an account that best suits your needs. For businesses you must use your corporate initials as your username. The username you select can be used as your account name, and this is how people discover you on Snapchat with the username you pick.

Here's how to set up an account:

* Start the Snapchat application and click "Sign Up.'

Enter your name, first and last and click 'Sign in and accept.'

Enter a birth date and then tap 'Continue.'

Create a username for your account that will represent your business or brand. The usernames that are available will be suggested when the one you'd like is not available. Be cautious when choosing the username since it cannot be changed in the future and the only method to alter the username is to create an account with a different one.

* Make a password and select 'Continue.'

Enter your email address and click "Continue.'

Check your balance using your telephone number. Press 'Continue' and then look for the verification code via text message. Input the code after receiving it and press 'Continue.'

Snapchat can only allow an account to be created per address. After you have created your account, you'll have to then create an avatar, and add friends.

Create a Profile Photo

After you have set up an account then the second step will be to set up an ID for your image. It is possible to create an avatar known as Bitmoji. It is a Bitmoji that can be used not just as a profile image but also as personalized stickers that you can incorporate into Snap content. Snap content.

Your profile picture is the fastest way for Snapchat users to find you on Snapchat.

* Tap the profile-photo icon at the left side in the camera's screen.

* Tap "Create Bitmoji"

Bitmoji is a no-cost avatar application that works with Snapchat and lets you make a cute, animated image for the profile. Your Bitmoji represents your digital image that you can share on Snapchat and will be displayed within your Snapcode.

Add Friends

The next step is add friends to your account, both from the contacts you have and, more importantly, those who aren't the new ones. It is possible to do this manually or allow the app to access your contacts list to allow you to select the people you want to include.

You might want to add your past clients as well as any potential clients to your list of contacts. To add someone to your list simply click the plus icon next to their name.

How do you add new Friends

Method 1: Through Snapcode

* Snap a photo of the individual's Snapcode or screen record it.

* Click on the ghost icon in the left-hand side of the screen.

* Choose 'Add Friends.'

* Choose Snapcode to start the roll of your camera.

* Choose the picture of the Snapcode from the camera roll.

* The picture will be taken and scanned. Your new friend will be added to your.

Method 2. By Username

You can use this method if you have the username of your friend. Find the username.

* Click on the ghost icon located at the left-hand corner.

* Click 'Add Friends.'

Select Username.'

Enter the username, then press"+" (Add) button below their name.

If you prefer go to the "Add Friends screen, you can email your user name to friends , so they can add you on their side.

Step Three: Create Nearby

This is best used for occasions so that you can add people you meet and interact with. meet. This allows you to include a variety of friends.

* Click on the ghost icon in the left-hand side of the screen.

* Click 'Add Friends.'

Choose 'Nearby.'

Click 'OK' and your Snapchat username will be displayed to Snapchat users that are near.

* Nearby Snapchat users who have their "Add Nearby" feature active, will be scanned before being displayed for you to select from.

* To add friends, click on the plus (Add) icon on the right side of that username. person you'd like to add.

* You must enable or enable location access settings in your Snapchat account to allow this feature to work.

4. Quick Add

It is also possible to use the "Quick Add" feature that suggests contacts you might like to connect to based on your the mutual contacts as well as other contacts on your phone. It may not work until you have started creating an Snapchat network.

* Click the ghost icon located at the left-hand side of the screen.

* Click 'Add Friends.'

* Scroll down until you see "Quick Add'

* Click on" + (Add) option next to each contact you wish to add.

Accepting a Friend Request from Snapchat

You must take a friend's request before you can be connected.

* Click on the ghost icon in the left-hand side of the screen.

* Click 'Add Me.'

* Click"+" (Add) button next to the username of the friend to grant the friend request.

Change Your Privacy Settings

To access your settings, go to your page on your profile. Click on the Bitmoji icon located at the top in the image screen.

* Click on the gear icon located on the upper right-hand corner of your screen to change your settings.

* Change settings as needed in the section 'Who Can.

You are able to modify these areas as follows:

* Contact people can be made.

* Settings for stories.

* Location.

Snapchatting

Snap is a Snap is direct messages sent on Snapchat from one individual to a friend or a group of friends. Snaps disappear after viewing and may be video or photo.

In the case of Snapchat marketing There are a variety of options and methods that you can employ to create marketing content.

To create content, press the large button at bottom of the page to snap the Snap.

After you've got a photo and you've got a picture, you can swipe it right or left based on what you wish to accomplish.

There are a variety of editing tools that are available on Snapchat to edit your videos and photos.

Making and editing Snaps

There are a variety of editing options available to make use of before you send the photo or video taken. Here are some of them:

Snaps

The app's launch will take you to the camera screen, where you are able to begin taking photographs. Make sure your camera is focused on what you want to capture and then tap the circle at the bottom of the screen. By holding that circle for a longer period, it will trigger the app to begin recording the video.

There's a symbol on the lower left-hand side of your smartphone that displays an upward-facing arrow. Clicking on it after taking your image will save the picture to the gallery of your phone so that you can look it up later.

Drawing on the back of a Snap

Modify your text by adding it your image , or drawing directly on screen using the draw tool . There is a the variety of colors to select.

Click the pen icon to activate the pen that is digital and drag your fingers across the display. Select the color you prefer by sliding your fingers across the color indicator.

The addition of text to a snap

If you want to add captions on your Snap you need to tap the 'T' symbol and add whatever you'd like to. You can expand and alter the location to ensure that the caption is the way you want it to appear.

Tap the 'T' symbol to add the text you want to add to your Snap The keyboard will appear where you can write an appropriate caption for the image.

Add stickers to Snaps Snap

You can add stickers by pressing the notepad icon. This will open the gallery of cute illustrations and images. Stickers can be used to mark your photos.

Making Stickers with Your Snap

You can make your personal sticker using the Snap Snap by pressing the scissors icon. This will cut off a part of the Snap and then paste it on the Snap Snap or another.

Linking to your Snaps

Additionally, you can use Snapchat's Snapchat Link feature in the form of a paperclip to connect an URL to your content . it will be available to your followers by swiping up on Snapchat. Snap.

To include a link in your Snaps it is necessary to create a new snap whether it's a video or photo.

Clicking the paperclip icon will bring you to a search bar that allows you to enter a URL for a website and then attach the URL to the Snap so that viewers can visit.

The ability to attach URLs to Snaps is an ideal solution for businesses who want to advertise their websites or blogs.

Timing Snaps

It is possible to alter the amount of time that an image spends hanging on the screen of a user or how long a movie plays. The timer icon is located on the left lower of your screen that can be tapped to set the limit of time to an image. The time you select is the duration you will be able to look at an image.

Click at the icon for stopwatch to alter the length of the Snap. The duration ranges from one second up to 10 seconds, or you can choose the infinity option, which means that anyone can see the Snap until the moment he or she decides to delete it.

The timer allows users to choose how often the video loops on the screen of a viewer before the Snap closes.

Addition of Snapchat Filters to Snap Snap

There are many filters on Snapchat including time, temperature, current speed, weather etc. If you would like to add these features in a Snap then you can swipe to the left or left to go to the filters options on the screen preview.

Change Filters

Once you've taken your image, you can switch the filters quickly by sliding left or right, as described earlier. The filter will then be visible on the image.

It is also possible to add an additional filter after you've applied one. Press and hold your screen, while moving left or right using a different finger.

There are a variety of filters to choose from For example, if you wish to make your photo to have blue tones or give it a vintage look There are filters available to help you achieve this. You can also use filters that display locations, however they're only available in specific regions or at specific dates.

Add Snapchat Lenses

If you tap the Snapchat screen prior to taking photos, you will be able to use Snapchat lenses. Alongside the usual smiley faces and bunny ears, lenses, there are also ones with virtual reality avatars and brand-sponsored lenses. Snapchat is currently testing AR-related content, such as that produced by artists.

Snapchat lenses are animated images that you can overlay onto your photos. This is the most thrilling feature for the majority of Snapchat users. It puts the appearance of a mask to your face whenever you take photos.

Snapchat lenses are among the most popular and used Snapchat features that can be utilized for marketing purposes for brands.

The feature also lets you to design your own lenses that are sponsored by you which offers the advantage of creating a lens that your followers can interact with and allow your brand to be more noticeable to your followers, as well as to the Snapchat users all around.

Lenses are pictures that show an impressive floral crown around their heads, glasses or even large rabbit ears over their heads or even having a mustache. The lenses make an app more enjoyable to play with and allow you to play for hours with lenses.

If you are looking to make your feed attractive to your viewers, think about adding these lenses to increase the excitement of your feed for viewers. Include one of these lenses when you post details on the app.

To make use of them, launch the app and make sure you make sure that the camera in front of you is pointed at you , so you are able to clearly see yourself. Click on your face, then hold it for a few seconds. The app will recognize your face and you'll see a grid that highlights the facial features. Release your grip.

After the mesh has been created you will see a number of lenses visible over the button to capture. These are tiny circle icons which you can slide around to explore the different effects, and then select one you like.

It is possible to take pictures and videos using the virtual masks. They can alter your appearance and also the surroundings of your picture. Save the photos and send them to your Snapchat acquaintances.

In order to submit your sponsored lens the creation you submit must be in line with the guidelines of the platform for advertising.

Making Snaps Geofilters by adding Geofilters

Find out which Geofilters are available in your area, since engaging with them will give you an increased reach. There is the option of purchasing Geofilters. Snapchat offers on-demand Geofilters to both individuals and businesses to buy.

Geofilters are filters specifically designed for specific locations. They are suitable for use in an event, business or other place. Brand logos and trademarks are also possible to be added.

Keep a Snap to Memories

Snaps don't last for long and are deleted when the people you share them with or they disappear within 24 hours if they are added to your Stories. You can however save your Snap permanently to Memories so that it can be seen in your phone's gallery of photos.

Remove the snap Snap

Another alternative is to erase the snap in case you don't like the photo; just click to return to the camera's screen so that you are able to take a fresh Snap.

Sending Snaps

Remember that once you upload the image the photo, it is not re-usable. If you want to save the image to be able to view later make sure you save it first.

Send the image using the arrow icon that is located on the lower right-hand corner of your screen. Once you have the Snap ready you can tap the'send-snap-1 icon in the lower-right on the Snap.

This icon will lead you to an overview of all of your friends. Choose the person you wish to share your photo with, then click the white arrow at the right-bottom of the friends list to send the Snap. A email will be sent out to the individual friends who you've shared an Snap.

Accessing Snapchat Content Snapchat

You can view various content of other users via the app. To access the content, swipe left. This will bring your to the Friends screen. You can view the their content here. It's obviously an intimate page that is not in your best interests.

If your intention is to utilize the app for marketing having more social posts might not be helpful for you. You can choose having a more professional interface that you can access by simply swiping left. This will take you to an overview screen that will display information that is more professional. You will discover articles from other brands and stories that are well-known.

This is a fantastic way to filter out information that you like. You will be aware of upcoming trends and discover what people are interested in. This information can later transfer to your own account to achieve more results. This is the way to keep yourself up to date with the world of Snapchat.

How to view the Snap sent to you

To see the Snap that was sent to you, simply swipe left on the screen of your camera to view your friends' list. If someone has sent an Snap direct to you there will be an indicator in the shape of a color-coded square to right of their name.

A red square signifies an image that is still Snap A purple square signifies the video, and a blue circle indicates text messages. Tap once to play or play the Snap. A number of Snaps of one person can be displayed as an album.

Additional Tips for Seeing Snaps

Click the screen one time to skipping the Snap or an Snap in the form of a Story.

* Scroll down until you exit.

There's two methods to view the Snapchat Story:

* On Your Friends list.

* On Your Discover page.

The Viewing Snapchat Stories from your Friends List

Click left on the camera's screen to view your list of friends and read the stories of your friends. Anyone who has shared an article will display an indicator on right of their name.

Click on the circle icon near a friend's profile to access their story. If you'd like to see your own Story open it by clicking on your profile icon in the upper left corner of the list of friends you have.

The ability to view Snapchat Stories from Your Discover Page

Like the name of the page suggests, it is where you can find Snaps and Stories. Here, you can see Stories from all of your friends , regardless of how you communicate with them.

To go to on the Discover Page, swipe left twice to view all your users with a current story. Stories are available for 24 hours, unless they are removed and you are able to view them as often as you want during that time.

"For You" Section

This section is located under Friends Stories. It is where you can discover the branded Snapchat Stories from businesses and marketers using Snapchat Business accounts.

* Swipe left to skip onto the next Story.

* Scroll down until you exit.

Editing and Adding Videos

In order to add videos,, press and hold the button for a while until the circle surrounding it glows as you record video footage. Press the release button until it stops. The video will then play and allow you to edit it like you would with a still image. Additional features are available to apply to videos, such as filters.

You can modify the videos that you upload to Snapchat. It lets you speed-forward the video, change it slow or even reverse it. These options can help make your video more engaging for viewers and bring more people to watch it.

To use the different options, first take your video, then move your finger left and right for access to the choices. There are a variety of icons to help you navigate through the different options.

The snail icon represents the slow-motion feature and will show your video running the slowest speed.

The rabbit icon signifies the option of fast forwarding that makes everything move more efficient within the movie.

Rewind is represented by a backwards-pointing forward arrow. It makes things occur in reverse. For instance, if there was a ball you kicked to the side, it will play in rewind mode, showing the ball returning to your hands.

Snapchat Emojis

There are Emojis available through Snapchat that are only accessible to you as a Snapchat user. They are usually displayed alongside some of the names you have given to your acquaintances. There's the smile emoticon, the smirk emoji sunglasses emoji and fire Emoji among other.

These Emojis typically show different levels of interaction with the Snapchat friends. For instance, a smile signifies a friend who snaps you often, but they don't actually snap all that often.

For business accounts the rules aren't applicable to you in the same way as they would for personal accounts. But, you can utilize it to increase interaction by noting people who constantly snap your photos, encouraging people to provide feedback and organizing contests.

Snapchat Stories

Snapchat Stories are quite different from snaps that are sent to people. Individual snaps typically disappear after a couple of seconds of viewing them. Snapchat stories however tend to last longer than a couple of seconds.

To share an Snapchat Story, tap on the icon that looks like the shape of a square that has the plus sign. Then, take the video or image you'd like to publish. Alternately, press the arrow icon in the bottom left of your screen after you have taken the picture, then tap on "My Story" in the upper right. The photo as well as the video into your feed.

Snapchat stories are often a series of pictures that you share every day. They are ideal to use when you're promoting an event, so you could create a series of images and videos that showcase the inside of the event, and let the viewers see the process behind the planning process to make them more excited about the occasion.

Stories typically last for 24 hours, after which they go away. The audience can watch them as often they like until the time of 24 hours is finished, and then they'll disappear.

When creating content for sharing on your feeds, make sure that you're confident in the content you are sharing. It is possible to try several times and then share only the content that is most appealing. The post will be online for 24 hours, so make sure it doesn't reflect your company's image negatively.

The Snap can be added to your Story

You can make an Story using a picture and/or video in your Story and only. The Snapchat Story will be available to all of your friends throughout the day.

After you have finished editing your Snap Select My Story to save the photo to your Story. The edited image will now be included in your story. Follow the same procedure to add other content to include by clicking the button to capture and editing another Snap before including it in your Story.

Making a Story from several videos or photos that are subsequently shown as a story to be seen by a larger public.

The process of creating Stories Story is similar to the steps to create an Snap as described above. When you're ready to publish your Story, save the Snap to "My Story,"" that is where you share it with your Facebook friends, or "Our Story" that adds the Snap to the other Stories that have been posted on Snapchat by fellow Snapchatters during the same time or in the same location.

The Story will be displayed on the Followers' Story timeline where they will be able to view your Snaps chronologically, in the order in which they were posted.

Travel Mode

Snapchat is a demanding app in terms of battery life and data usage. Snapchat consumes a significant amount of battery and data when it's in use. Your battery could be drained quicker when the app is running. To prevent this from happening, Snapchat has a 'Travel Mode function that addresses this problem.

Travel mode helps preserve your battery's life and is an integrated function of Snapchat. When you enable it you can stop the automatic download of images and videos every time you launch the app. It will, in turn, reduce battery usage and data. When you set your application into travel mode you will be able to select the snaps you want to load and which ones to not load.

To switch to the travel mode option Open your application, then tap the ghost icon that is located in the middle of the display. There will be the gear icon, which you can tap. You can turn to the Travel Mode and you're good to go.

Here are a few of the features and features of Snapchat which will help you have the ability to navigate the application. It's quite simple once you understand how to use it. Test it out and utilize the different options to make the most of it. Digitalize your marketing and be ahead of the curve.

We will explore ways you can utilize Snapchat to market in the next section.

Chapter 6: Tips To Use Snapchat To Help With Business And Marketing

There are around 200 million active Snapchat users. In addition around 700 million images and videos are uploaded on a daily basis with more than 500 million views every day.

These numbers suggest an enormous potential audience for anyone who is interested in using the application for marketing purposes and, most crucially, for anyone who is looking to expand the reach of their app.

It could be exhausting to consider the next social platform that you could add to the list of social media platforms that you already promote your services or products. But those numbers as well as the opportunities they provide cannot be ignored.

It is recommended to utilize any platform that offers new and better ways to reach out to your prospective clients and existing customers of your business. These Snapchat figures are incredibly attractive and ought to have you thinking about ways to integrate Snapchat in your advertising plan.

Additionally, we are aware that Snapchat is distinct from other social networks because of its niche young people who make Snapchat distinct. Strategies employed will differ in addition to the target audience and expectations. Based on the strategy you choose it could be a benefit or disadvantage.

Snapchat because of its popularity and the kind of users it can attract can be a crucial element for marketing strategies. While it is often employed for personal use Snapchat can be employed in business and may even make you money and help market your brand.

Snapchat is definitely a great platform that every company should consider using and incorporate into their marketing plans to grow followers naturally or to use for paid advertising since it's growing quickly both for personal and professional use.

How to Begin

1. Create a personal Snapchat Account

Begin with your Snapchat advertising campaign with your own account. Begin by adding family and friends and then expanding to following the accounts that your ideal people might be following. The reason you should create an account on your own for people who are brand new to Snapchat is to assist you get acquainted with the platform.

It was found that the top performing marketing content is comparable to the native content created by the typical Snapchat user. Also, try to make your content as personal as you can. Utilize filters, Emojis as well as doodles, and continue to publish Snaps. The more frequently you post and the more engaged your followers are more likely you are of achieving success in marketing.

2. Create an account on Snapchat for your business. Snapchat Business Account

Once you've mastered the basics of Snapchat, and you have mastered the basics of Snapchat using your personal Snapchat account Next step is to sign up for Business accounts.

Sign in to Snapchat and complete the registration form, providing the following information:

* Business name

* Your name

* Business email address

* Business place

* Currency; dollars, pounds, etc.

Then go through the steps to connect your business Snapchat profile to your own Snapchat account in order to create your personal page.

3. Plan a Marketing Success Measurement Plan

You should be able evaluate your progress and achievement through the creation of a measurement strategy.

Snapchat performance focuses on:

* Retention rate - The percent of viewers who have watched all of your stories and allows you to evaluate the viewership of the entire Story in order to figure out which performs better.

For instance, the best length of a video has been determined as 90 minutes. The majority of people are bored when videos are longer than 90 seconds.

* Analytics can help you determine how many viewers are not following the story after the 2nd Snap and will give you an idea of the overall attention to the story. The most common rule is when 30% of viewers quit watching following the 2nd Snap then the Story may not be that efficient.

• Review the feedback of your followers to gain an understanding of your performance. One way to gauge feedback towards success is having your followers comment that they enjoy your content.

4. Get Your Team Involved to participate in Snapchat Creation of Content Creation and Ideas

The process of creating content can be difficult for one person to accomplish effectively. It's best to get other people involved to assist you with your creativity and ideas for creating captivating content. Engage your team from work or your family and friends to help with creating content to promote your business on Snapchat.

5. The focus is on Variety of Content

Monotony can be boring. It's not truer for marketing on social media which is a place where people are always looking for fresh and interesting content , and you need to keep a step ahead to keep your customers or viewers engaged.

For keeping your fans interested make sure you regularly publish interesting content is an effective way to do this. Snapchat users are looking to read information in various formats, so make sure that you make use of the many innovative apps available that are available on Snapchat.

Content variety can be obtained through the interplay of concepts and formats. For instance:

* Graphics/Drawing/Emojis

* Video/Images/Photos

* Selfie-style video/Point and Shoot video

* Sound/Silent

Try out different kinds of content to determine which will draw and draw the attention of the audience the most.

6. Create a unique approach to increase your Fans

Snapchat unlike other social media platforms, requires users to think outside the box in order to build a following, and maintain the momentum. Utilize other channels of brands such as blog posts or social media to gain followers to your profile.

Also, create plans for the long-term to promote your business and your page to ensure that you are able to keep attracted to new followers while also engage those you already have. Get involved with influencers and other your partners by including your page on their accounts and then letting them spread the news about your brand among their fans. The best method of increasing followers is by engaging them and participating in the conversation.

7. Don't be a perfectionist.

Making sure everything is perfect is not the best method to approach Snapchat since the content you post should be a bit off the wall. Try to be as authentic as you can without excessive editing or tasks that go to create your content. The more authentic your material, the more captivating and fascinating your Stories will be.

The audience

Instagram is a highly attractive market. The characteristics of its users are fascinating, since we find that a large portion, or more than half of the users of the app are between 13 and 34 years old in the US who have access to smartphones.

The target audience Snapchat offers is mostly younger users. The majority of users are younger than 25 years old. of age. Your intended audience will guide your marketing plan. If you're trying to attract the'millennials and millennials, then Snapchat is a great choice for you.

Snapchat Marketing Strategies

Snapchat is distinct than other media sites. It is therefore not possible to apply the same strategies that you employ for other platforms for Snapchat. It is necessary to develop different strategies specifically designed to this app.

Remember that with Snapchat it is only sharing photos and videos with specific people and sharing images or videos. You don't have social proof because you are not able to retain communication with other users, or even have them commenting on your post that you posted just a few days ago.

Through this application, it is about bringing your content to those who are actually interested with it. Engaging more users by bringing new content out every day is the aim so you need to plan with this idea in the back of your mind.

There are strategies that have been tried and proven to be effective for other companies that have been marketed using the same platform in the past. These techniques continue to be effective up to date. These comprise:

1. Influencer Marketing

Popular people who utilize Snapchat as celebrities are likely to have a huge influence over others Snapchat users.

Consider the case of a pop star who wrote negative comments about Snapchat after the platform had altered some of its features . It resulted in the platform losing billions of dollars due to the ripple effect it created.

Influencers are a crucial element of marketing and can create a huge impact. You'll need to collaborate with an influencer in order to increase your followers and boost the amount of sales you make.

To collaborate with influencers, you'll first have to identify influential people who align with your brand. Then, join them in your marketing campaign. The influencers may work in different methods, so you are able to pick one or all based on the method you believe will be the most effective for your business.

a)Full Takeover

This kind of route is when the influencer has control the control of the account Snapchat profile for a certain period of time in the example of one day or half a day. They then post snaps to the account.

In order to make this strategy work for you, you must create a large amount of advertisements in advance on all other social networks , as well as Snapchat itself.

The ads will aim around informing your followers of the influencer takeover , and also making them excited so that on the day of the event, they're all eagerly anticipating the event. Invite your influencer to promote the takeover and get certain followers along with them.

Therefore, this kind of strategy is ideal to be used when there's an event and you could ask the person who is influential to share Snaps of them and other attendees at your event.

If, for instance, there is an open-day for people to get more information on your service, you could include a local musician who can entertain the crowd during the event. The artist could post photos on your Instagram account prior to the event, showing what's taking place behind the scenes in preparation for the event.

It will get people talking about the event and could result in you having a more people out, possibly leading to higher sales towards close of day, as well as in the future.

It is essential that you speak with the influencer before hand about the type of content they may share on your account. Be sure throughout the promotion that your brand and products are highlighted. There are discounts on specific products.

It is also possible to have takeovers become a regular event that occurs once two weeks, when there are different influencers join your account. This keeps your account interesting and fresh and allow you to connect with various social networks through influencers.

This approach has some drawbacks. For instance you're limited to the existing audience you have as your followers. You are only able to do enough to make an influencer announce and spread to their followers. That might not produce the most effective outcomes.

b)Sponsored Posts

This is typically more effective than the complete takeover and solves the issue of having a small public. This particular method is where you can have influencers who collaborate with to promote your content through their own accounts.

Once you've identified influential people whose followers are in line with your market segment Reach out to them and suggest a partnership proposal to them. You can then collaborate with the influencers on coming up with content that you can publish on their pages.

You'll need to contribute some money to support influencer marketing, however because the posts last only all day on Snapchat you don't have to pay the same amount as other social media platforms like Instagram as well as Facebook.

The sponsored posts must be authentic and not forced. Involving the influencers in the creating content is the best. This will let them offer their opinion on what's more natural to them.

Also, ensure that the influencer is featured in the video or image. This strengthens the relationship with the person who is in charge and your company.

In addition to having an influencer associated with your product, they should also be able to provide written content they can contribute to further promoting your brand and products.

Consider discounts as well to your influential person. The followers will increase their interest in the idea of buying your product.

If you've got different influencers throughout time, using discounts also allows you to track how well each influencer are performing by taking into account the sales that are generated through promotional codes. These data are crucial for future strategies since you will know which influencer to choose to follow in the near future.

Be aware that influencer campaigns don't always produce immediate sales. However, having a well-known person who promotes your content can increase the likelihood for followers to be aware of your brand. They'll think about your brand's image when making purchase decisions.

Be aware that there might not be a immediate need for the services you provide, but they could come up later.

Simple as a paid shout-out to your brand's name from an influencer can be beneficial for marketing purposes and doesn't cost anything if you're operating on a tight budget.

Here are some helpful suggestions to use for sponsored posts:

* They must be authentic. It is suggested to let the influencer shoot the picture on their own to ensure that it looks as natural as is possible.

* The influencer should appear in the photo in order to reinforce their relationship with your brand and to show their endorsement of it.

* The influencer must have a distinct discount code for the product or service they are promoting to ensure that their followers are enticed to purchase the item or service. Discount codes for influencers aid in monitoring the effectiveness of the influencer's campaign.

The benefit of the influencer-based marketing approach is, even when outcomes may not be immediate their endorsement of your company automatically increases the probability of their fans buying.

2. Create Anticipation

Snapchat is particularly useful for sharing behind-the-scenes preparations for an occasion. It typically does not require professional photography since even unretouched photos and videos can be posted. This allows you to generate excitement by with the app for your followers and others.

Release sneak peeks of the event prior to it happening. Short videos that end with a cliffhanger to make the audience want to go to the event and experience the event firsthand.

Make use of your photos to tell stories in preparation for the event itself.

Utilize phrases and information that leave viewers wanting to know more. Use phrases such as "Just wait for the biggest reward we're waiting for.' It is also possible to start an countdown of days leading up to the big event to increase excitement.

3. Constant Interaction

It is essential to keep a regular contact with your followers, by posting images and videos every day every day without failing. The reason for this is that it helps to keep your brand's name in the minds of your followers and gives them fewer chances of forgetting about your brand's name if they can are able to see it every time they use the application.

These daily snapshots to provide more details about your products and show their everyday use by short videos. For daily content you can also include various features, brand new product announcements as well as behind-the-scenes footage as well as videos about the use for the products you sell.

Make use of Snapchat editor tools to create entertaining and engaging material for the followers of yours.

This is useful when combined alongside other strategies that aim at growing your followers, such as influencer marketing. Combine these strategies to attract new followers and maintain the ones which you currently have.

Establish a sense of familiarity with your company to your customers so they consider your brand first when they need the product you have to offer.

4. Snap Ads

Snapchat Ads are a great option for marketing your business and investing in the feature is worth every penny for small and large companies. Snap Ads are displayed via the story function. sometimes, users will get an ad to appear when they read an article.

In comparison to a social media site such as Facebook Advertising on Snapchat is superior because ads have a longer lead times, Ad specifications are more precise, and they are also more cooperative with Snapchat's platform.

Snap Ads are able to reach the same audience as regular photos in the form of videos that can run up to 10 seconds in length. Snap Ads permit you to connect directly to a site or add attachments to your viewers to download or download through the app and publish videos. Snap Ads offer more creative possibilities than other platforms that have features like filters.

5.Snapchat Promotions

The primary goal of this method is to boost the sales of e-commerce. It is ideal to have a large following since you'll be able to be more widely known.

Through these promotions there are discounts and coupon codes on certain days that are only available to Snapchat users. You can also promote coupons prior to their release on other social media platforms in order to make sure that more people know about the promotions and build your following this way.

To promote the promo code, first post your photo or video telling tell the story of your company or the product that you are selling, along with the promotion code and an URL to your site.

Then, ask your audience to capture the photo and then share it on their social media accounts too. Then, give the code to people who share their snaps and share it to their stories.

It is also possible to encourage your followers to share pictures and videos of them wearing your product and receive discounts on your product. This specific move will enable you to gain access to user-generated content that works great to promote your business and enhance the interaction between your customers and you.

Coupon codes let you acquire content you can later share via user-generated content. They can also create a sense urgency for customers as they feel pressured to buy something quickly before the offer runs out.

Increase the urgency of this offer by reminding viewers of the remaining time until the coupon expires. There are one-day coupons, or ones that run for several hours or even days.

The coupon codes are tracked, which means you are in a position to monitor the number of people who purchase purchases or take advantage of your promotion. Then, you can use this data to design future campaigns and modify your promotional strategies to suit your needs.

The need to have a trackable and measurable marketing strategy is what makes coupon codes crucial to be aware of what your Snapchat marketing strategies are performing. The tracking of data on Snapchat isn't easy, so coupon codes can help in this particular area.

6. Sponsored Filters

Snapchat allows users to buy filters. Users can now purchase a Snapchat filter to modify it, and then allow it to be shared with others for a predetermined period of time.

Companies can make use of sponsored filters to add features like logos , and add a funny accent to Snapchat images and videos.

Snapchat collaborates with businesses to design custom filters to advertise their brand and have proved beneficial to businesses that have already benefited from the feature.

It is now possible to create Interactive filters that you can use for your Snapchat followers to use for promotion purposes. This interactive and fun form of marketing is unique and different from traditional advertising , which makes it more entertaining and efficient.

7. Geofilters Sponsored by Geofilters

Snapchat Geofilters are essentially geo-based filters, which are images that users can apply over drawings and images that they include on their Snapchat snaps. Geofilters can be made using stickers, images, or captions that the user chooses to share on the snap.

Geofilters have proven to be extremely efficient in attracting new businesses. They let users select your Geofilter in the location of their choice after they have taken an Snap and then make use of your location filters in order to describe exactly where and when you took the Snap took place, the reason it was taken and at what time the snap was captured.

Geofilters can detect the location of users and allow users to stamp on the Snap to inform followers of their location as well as what they're doing at the place. Are you in business? For business? Snapchat filters for occasions you're planning; for special occasions, for launches of products, or to simply display the day-to-day operations of your company.

Sponsored Geofilters can be simpler to develop than Snap Ads, and they are a low-cost advertising tool that can be based on the location of your choice. They are great for enticing customers and fans to share their brand and store experiences with their networks.

Geofilters are like lenses, but aren't as interactive and are location-specific. When you create Geofilters by creating a Geofilter and choose a specific area where it will broadcast, and the duration you wish it to run. When a person who follows you receives the Geofilter, they can add your geofilter to their pictures and videos and share it with friends; thus increasing your exposure and brand's visibility. This also encourages customer or service engagement.

Due to the personal interaction Snapchat provides, Geofilters can have a significant role to play in developing relationships with customers in organic development. Geofilters typically have a company logo, but can be used for everything that's in line with Snapchat's guidelines.

Geofilters are crucial to promote an event and generate excitement about the event. If you are hosting an event you're planning to be hosting, you can ask your followers to take advantage to the geofilter. Take photos using the Geofilter to promote your event and post them to their social media.

Make sure to share this event to your favorite social networks as and provide information on the Geofilter. Be aware that people should be aware of it to be able to look it up. Don't waste your money by buying an Geofilter that nobody knows about.

When you've created awareness of this event as well as the Geofilter, Snapchat users should begin to search for and use the Geofilter. This could increase the number of people who are aware of that event. It could make it easier for more people to turn at the event.

Geofilters are also great to spread the news about your business's new venture even if you're just beginning one. This will help to boost your business's growth as it allows you to connect with the people's families and friends as well as the benefit of trust between the person who posts a photo as well as their friends.

They'll be more accepting to new products using this method as opposed to if you advertise directly to them. According to data from Snapchat the National Sponsored Geofilter can reach an average of 40-60 percent of Snapchatters who use it daily across the US.

You may ask users who are using the Geofilter to include the terms of your URL or handle to their captions of text. This will allow them to identify your company to those who are interested.

Geofilters are a hit with the younger generation due to the fact that it's essentially an improvement of text-based tags; they create Snaps more expressive , by offering exclusive access to specific business activities as well as the location. Geofilters allow the sharing of content more easily in the limits of a location filter.

Sponsored Geofilters can be compared to words of mouth sales pitches People are more likely to believe the opinions and experiences of people they know prior to making purchases. Geofilters can help connect your ads to user experience.

8. Sponsored Lenses

Snapchat lenses are animated images created by the camera's selfie view. They trigger by facial expressions such as smile, kiss open mouth, raised eyebrows. The most well-known lenses include:

* Angelic facial features.

Face of a dog: nose, ears and tongue.

* Vomit rainbow.

The purpose lens's goal is to create content as entertaining as is possible. Lenses that are sponsored are typically the result of a partnership with Snapchat and the marketing company; you supply design elements and a storyboard . Snapchat creates your lens.

Lenses can be very engaging and easily visible. As such they are a great way for businesses to sponsor lenses that are utilized by followers to share videos and photos. Snapchat states that users of the app will engage with the lens for minimum 20 seconds, and then share content using the lens.

9. Snapchat Discover

Snapchat Discover is a corporate feature which has been around at the very beginning of the year and is a distinct aspect of Snapchat. Discover is corporates and big companies publish their marketing stories.

Similar to Snapchat Stories, Discover Stories also include audio-video and picture content, which is coupled with graphics and articles. Within Discover is the online retail store that was that was launched by Snapchat in the year 2018. At present, it carries only Snapchat products, but it is able to expand into an in-app marketplace that allows other companies to sell.

10. Bitmoji

Snapchat through its partnership with Bitmoji has created the possibility for companies to design personal avatars for their brand that they can use to market your company through the platform. A mascot or avatar in your stories or content can personalize your brand as well as make it more memorable and more relatable to.

Strategy for Marketing: What can you do to make the most value from Snapchat

Strategies involve considering what content would be most effective for your marketing strategy on Snapchat. It is essential to develop an the ability to implement a plan of action to be able to connect and increase the number of people who follow you.

To achieve the most benefit from marketing through Snapchat you must have a well-defined strategy and experience to use Snapchat effectively to attract users to your brand and turn them into customers. It is essential to understand who the person using Snapchat is to succeed. You need to determine people who use the system and the way they use it.

A successful marketing campaign takes patience and a thorough plan for success Marketing via

Snapchat requires you to make use of your company's distinctive selling point.

We will go over the different Snapchat marketing strategies and how you can get the most value from these strategies. Let's begin with the most important steps to follow to create a successful Snapchat plan of marketing:

Step 1: Conduct research and understand Snapchat User Profiles and Demographics

Each social network is different. Snapchat marketing is not viewed in the same manner like Facebook or Instagram because there are specific marketing aspects that are specific to Snapchat and require to be treated in the same way. For example, the dominant age group of Snapchat users is different from the majority of the users who use Twitter Therefore, your strategies for marketing on Snapchat and Instagram cannot be the same.

The first step in implementing efficient and effective marketing using Snapchat is to learn about the users to ensure that you package your content to be appealing to the people who are there. You can ask the following questions:

What are frequent users and what type or content they prefer?

• Who's the main target audience?

* What is the average age according to the segments? The majority of the users (71% are under the age of 31.

What is the gender breakdown? One in 10 users on Snapchat are female.

When you have numbers estimates and a clear division of the audience on Snapchat You will be able to determine what you can do to create your content to your intended audience. In general, Snapchat will serve your business best when you cater to women and the younger age group.

Based on the data you collect regarding the regular Snapchat users, you'll be able to understand how they interact with Snapchat and, in turn discover the best approach and mix to engage with them.

In your study, you'll realize that the typical Snapchat user doesn't invest long amounts of time per session on Snapchat however they check in and out many times throughout the day, using this time mostly for personal communications. Your message is likely to be seen by a wide audience, however, it must be designed to be appealing and engaging in order to be shared with these people.

Step 2 Step 2: Set Your Goals

After doing your research, determine the goals of marketing you wish to accomplish on Snapchat. The most important goal for every brand that is a subscriber through Snapchat is to boost engagement with their brand, especially in the demographic aged between 15 and 35 who comprise the largest users of Snapchat.

When your objectives are clearly defined and you're confident that the Snapchat users will assist you to meet your branding objectives then you can proceed onto the next stage which is to outline your strategy to marketing on Snapchat. It is then time to determine and establish the focus of your marketing and how you will do it.

Step 3: Determine and Decide the Marketing Focus and the Style of Snapchat

After you've done your research, you have to decide on what your marketing's focus is and how you'll create content that is appropriate for your group of customers. Once you've identified your target customers and determine the best way to present your content to appeal to them The following step is execute your plan to achieve the desired results.

Consider how you are planning to reach your Snapchat marketing objectives. Concentrate on the content that is going to resonate with the audience you are trying to reach. For instance, it's more effective to share fun pictures or videos featuring your brand's logo or product, rather than blatant advertising for a service or product. Being aware of what's trending will help you stay current with what your target audience is looking at to ensure your style of content remains relevant.

Remember that Snapchat is founded by having fun. Therefore your content must be compatible with the style of Snapchat. Don't try to impress through official messaging. Users on Snapchat want fun videos, filters, animations lenses, stickers and many other features, as well as including your brand's name, products or services.

Once you've got the two steps taken care of, the main aspect to be aware of when you are committing to Snapchat marketing is that there is no set formula to follow for success. Beyond the general rules and information you'll get in this book as well as elsewhere, Snapchat marketing is primarily about experimentation.

Test every method and approach until you finally settle on the best one for you. Make use of all the features available in your content and monitor the reaction of your audience - this can be the best way to be aware of what works best.

Know how different kinds of Ads operate, the subtleties of the delivery of messages, and the user experience that each offers.

While doing this you must implement your marketing plan by having a clear knowledge of your goals for marketing. The more people identify with and appreciates the marketing material and overall strategy the more effective it will be. However keep in mind that excessive advertising could damage your business.

Here are some crucial tips and tricks to help you develop your marketing strategy for your business Snapchat: Snapchat:

1. Create an online marketing theme

A successful marketing strategy must be able to convey a message through your stories; you should remain consistent with your message. The theme you choose should be based on your company's brand and your items or products.

Stories of your employees or a tutorial on your products or services, brand new product or development on the horizon, and so on. With a common thread throughout your communications, it's much easier for people to follow, engage and connect with your brand. It's also easier to promote your business if you've got clearly defined messages.

2. Do not duplicate content

You are aware that to succeed in online marketing the right content is essential. original and fresh content will win. Make sure you don't duplicate content from different platforms. make your Snapchat content stand out from your other channels for marketing.

The desire of copying and pasting content on one platform to the next i.e. Instagram Stories to Snapchat Stories and vice versa is not uncommon, but it will not work in the long run. Your followers won't need to go to the Snapchat website if you discover the same content they've observed in Facebook and Instagram. This is why you must create distinctive content that has a distinct and unique worth for each of your audience.

Your content must be suitable to Snapchat and your target audience on Snapchat as well as fun and exciting spur-of-the-moment snaps and stories are the best to use for Snapchat marketing. Better yet, take advantage of additional features for marketing such as Geofilters, Emojis, stickers, text captions that are multi-colored and more.

Make sure you share any important news or exclusive content to ensure your Snapchat followers get to enjoy exclusive content that nobody has ever seen before. In-depth glimpses into the production process and other intriguing insider info will keep your audience wanting more.

3. Genuine Content

Snapchat wants authentic content. That is the content should be authentic and current. All that's required for you to do is be imaginative to get the most out of your content. Users on Snapchat are looking for actual-time, real-time content instead of personalized Snapchats.

This is the place where your team will be crucial, as it can be difficult to produce an ongoing stream of genuine content. Engage your team members in this process and motivate them to create content to promote your products, business and services. This will not only guarantee an ongoing stream of new content however, it also creates an exciting blend of genuine content.

Your followers will feel that they are part of your company by sharing content they won't find elsewhere. Exclusive content sharing makes people feel special and creates an emotional connection to your brand as well as content. If you post exclusive content with Snapchat, you create a sense of belonging. Snapchat communities, you create the feeling of community and confidence with your business.

4. Create engaging and fun content

One of the key aspects of creating content that is engaging that is suitable for Snapchat Stories is to make the content entertaining to read. The best content should that it incorporates all of the Snapchat features and don't be afraid to play with your content.

Success on Snapchat is much more likely through personalized content that is a personal experience for the viewer or reader instead of a commercial pitch. Be yourself and share your stories and experiences or, at the very least, act as you're yourself and your audience will be awestruck.

Include in your marketing content interesting and educational moments, particularly on the form of Snapchat Stories, such as recording and sharing photos of your day-to-day business actions. Snapchat Stories are excellent marketing tools since they're typically low-cost and easy to make However, the ROI is high because they draw attention and keep your followers engaged.

5. Make Use of More Location-Based Features

Make sure to include more features that are based on location for the content of your Snaps and Stories because you will benefit from your brand even if don't have Stories built for your account as of yet. Geofilters and location features can allow you to share your experience in a particular event, or work place with followers.

You can use your Geofilters to highlight any event or promotion, or allow your followers and customers to share their experience. Snapchat offers on-demand geofilters to any user - they can use filters that they can customize to fit their images.

Geofilters are very affordable based on the Geofence, which is the space which is the area covered with the Geofilter. They also offer statistics to track how many people are viewing and use the filter.

What can you do to maximize the Benefits Geofilters

These are the proven methods to get the most value out of Geofilters to assist you with the success of your Snapchat promotion:

a. Create Engaging Geofilters

Like any other marketing material like other marketing content, Geofilters need to be designed to be interesting for the viewer. It's not just an issue of putting in your logo and hoping that the viewers will be thrilled by it. To get your followers excited to promote your Geofilters make them help enhance the user's Snap to make them inspired to spread the word about it.

b. Create Geofilters about Sharing Experiences

The most efficient method of getting the most benefit from Snapchat is to share your experiences. Geofilters can give your followers the chance to tell you the places they are in or what they're up to. In turn, you can share your experiences and experiences with followers.

C. Geofilters Are Most Effective when they are targeted

The most effective way to market online is targeted marketing. determine your target audience or niche and then create content for these people, including Geofilters. Geofilters can be extremely efficient and can be very effective for capturing people in a certain area, particularly if those targeted are present at an occasion.

Geofencing allows you to keep your followers follow you no matter regardless of where you are via informing platforms about where the filter is most effective geographically. Geofencing makes sure that the correct users have the ability to access your geofilter. Anyone who is within the bounds of your geofence will be alerted and is more likely to use the filter, and share the Snaps in their stories and also expose your brand's name to those who follow it.

For the most optimal results with Geofencing you should consider these suggestions:

* Geofencing comes with a limit of 50 square feet. For the most effective Geofencing functionality make sure that your Geofilter is set to an area of 20,000 square feet.

* To ensure adequate coverage, avoid using lots of circular points that have tiny spaces that hinder coverage.

6. Context Cards and Snap Maps

Snap Maps were first introduced in the mid-2017 period by Snapchat in mid-2017. It allows users to use Snap Maps which allow users to show their current location. Your company Bitmoji will be displayed on a map indicating the location you are in and also the option of opting-out.

Maps also assist you in identifying the areas near to you that you and your Snapchat buddies last took a snap from. The heat spots will show the locations where users are most likely to capture Snapchat content. Clicking on them, you'll find the photos that were taken in the areas highlighted within 24 hours.

In the same time, Snapchat added Context Cards on Snap Maps to give users context information on the area that the content displayed on the map originates from.

Context Cards will help you find more information about advertising through Snapchat by providing market data based on location, based on location.

Utilize Context Cards to inquire and invite your customers and your followers to share their experiences in your outlets or stores through geofilters for your location. Furthermore, fixed companies have now a distinctive way to reach their customers and their followers.

7. Start Small

This is a tried and tested strategy for any marketing strategy You should always begin at a low level and progress from there. Don't try to target too numerous marketing techniques, select only one or two developing them, and then improve them to ensure their success.

If you're successful with the first or two you've begun with, present the next. The best way to begin is to create a custom Geofilter for the next occasion such as a launch of a new product or a business event or tradeshow you're going to, or some other occasion that is special.

8. Create Brand Awareness and Increase Business Social Media Presence

Statisticians have shown how Snapchat is the most popular social media platform of the 12-24 age group with more than 150 million people active each day.

Create your own Snapchat account that you can use consistently and frequently to promote your company to connect with Snapchat users within your geographical region and let them know about your brand.

9. Make use of Influencers

As was mentioned in the past, using influencers is efficient in giving your followers and customers an inside view of your company through an influencer partnership to promote your brand's message through their Snapchat account or by letting the influencer the right to own your account. You can also work with an influencer that has followers comparable to your customers.

Work with famous people and famous people on social media as well as entertainers are the most effective to promote your brand due to their huge following. The exchange of accounts that have a persona that has this kind of status can be excellent for engagement with followers as your followers will be enthusiastic about it. Additionally, followers of the person, or his the genre of his or hers will be intrigued.

10. Coupons and Vouchers

Rewards and coupons work both online and on social media equally well as they do offline.

Promoting coupons through the website, your Snapchat account, website , and online store . You can send coupons to your customers who endorse your services and products via sharing the content via their accounts.

Snapchat offers features to create coupons you can distribute the coupons to those who follow you. You can also use contests or offer rewards to users who share the content of your company through Snapchat. Snapchat accounts.

Utilizing Snapchat to offer vouchers is advantageous for companies and the majority of Snapchat users would redeem them for discounts they can avail. Many college students would prefer discounts or special offers from the brands they follow on Snapchat and 58% of them are more likely to purchase something when they get coupons from Snapchat.

The excitement that comes with Snapchat messaging, coupled with the lure of a deal or savings through coupons or vouchers will encourage users to buy. Shoppers are enticed by the offers and leave with the unique feeling that they are part of an exclusive customer group who have access to discounts that which other customers aren't able to access.

Coupons and vouchers are simple to make. Make a snap of one that is physical or design one specially to be used on Snapchat. Share it with all your followers via posting your post through Snapchat Story. This will keep your followers to be accustomed to it , and they'll continue to check your posts to find the latest offers, and more importantly, word will get out to people who are unaware of the promotions offered through your brand, which can increase the number of followers you have.

11. Contests

Contests function in like vouchers and coupons that increase awareness of your brand, keep your customers and fans entertained, as well as to build greater brand recognition for your business.

If they are used in a proper manner If they are used correctly, contests can be the most effective incentive to encourage people on Snapchat to join and to engage on your page. The most effective contests solicit followers' Snaps that meet certain requirements in exchange for rewards. It could be that they provide the correct answer to a query, or upload a video or photo through one of the channels and share a picture or video of your product or when they purchase the service, etc.

When the contest time has finished, select the winners or your top photos or videos , based on the contest type and make the awards available at the address of the winner. You could also award the others who did not get prizes for consolation, such as coupons for discounts so that they feel as if they were winners. Distribute items that advertise your company's image.

Contests don't just bring excitement and awareness to your followers, but they can also assist in converting potential customers and make them more receptive to future sales. The principal reason to use competitions for marketing purposes is to maintain the people you win to increase sales and engagement in the future.

12. Snapchat Swap Takeovers

Similar to the influencer taking over your account. In Snapchat takeovers two Snapchat users switch accounts for 24 hours, and then take the opportunity to promote your brand's image to the new followers on the accounts they are taking over and keep existing followers on the account.

Takeovers can be a excellent way to increase the size of your audience and create an audience because you get the chance to collaborate and promote your brand to a larger crowd.

Most popular forms of takeovers to employ include:

* Celebrity takeovers

* Customer takeovers

* Employee takeovers

* Influencers take over

Through takeovers, you can have the possibility of sharing information via features such as:

* Broadcasting and broadcasting live events

"What a joke!" Snapchat antics

* Sessions for Question and Answer

* Doing "A A Day in the Life'

Before you launch a Snapchat acquisition, make sure you do the research to determine the successful brands that have used it in order to reap the benefits.

The best time to use them is at events such as launches and celebrations, awards, conference, seminars, sports tournaments , etc. They are most effective when they take place at the time of an event. For instance, if you organize an exchange takeover with a star actor at the Oscars and it is an amazing explosion. The actor's footage from behind the scenes of the show will create a great amount of engagement and the value of your brand for your followers and could draw more attention to your business.

As the actor takes control of your account, you'll be following the same process on his Snapchat account, and making use of the time to interact with the followers of his account while promoting your company.

Utilize as many of the Snapchat strategies as you can throughout the period of time that you are taking over to keep your people following you. In doing so, ensure that your content is engaging as well as fun and include marketing content about your services or products extensively but not in the center. This is a good time to introduce coupons, contests, vouchers and other promotions or even Q&As.

13. Snapchat Q&A Sessions

Q&A sessions are great for interacting participants, teaching, and gaining feedback from a brand or the products and services it offers. The purpose for Q&A is to build and maintain meaningful connections with customers and followers.

Create a Q&A on Snapchat to turn your followers into customers. It is crucial to involve them actively involved in the running of the event, by asking them to answer questions and provide suggestions of topics they would prefer to be discussing. Make sure that all information discussed in the Q&A section is relevant to or about your company's products, brand or services.

Tips to Ensure Success on Snapchat Snapchat Q&A

Be aware of the time limit. Remember that Snapchat videos can be only 10 seconds in length. Therefore the question and the answer should be presented in two snaps.

* Acknowledge the person who sent your question, and thank them for the contribution they made to the discussion. This gives them a sense of belonging and make them feeling more connected to your brand.

Engage the audience by walking through your office, shift to various locations within your city, engage others in your team and get your audience members to try and make guesses or anticipate the answers, etc. Create the most exciting experience possible. Prior to closing the event, you may offer discounts vouchers to people who took part or made contributions.

14. Consistency: Daily Snaps

Consistency is crucial in your messages to boost awareness for your business in addition to the knowledge of your products or services. Snaps from every day life have these advantages:

They're excellent to establish your brand's image within your customers' minds. It's easy. If they read and see about you each day They will not forget you . But, more important they will enjoy taking a look at your Snaps.

The fact that you take photos every day increases the value of your content because people expect more from your content. You'll need to upgrade your content and share more than your logo and photos of products. This will increase interaction and awareness about your company's brand.

Include events for business as well as other exciting events within every day Snaps. Consistent messages allow the user to update their customers of your business's activities as well as the products you sell, so, they become more aware of your company's image.

15. Inserting video ads into Live Stories

Make sure you include more video ads on Your Snapchat Stories. The data provided from Snapchat show that the site has 10 billion video clips watched by daily users. This means that there is an enormous demand and a preference for videos on Snapchat that you should benefit from.

Videos are appealing to the more than 200 million people who regularly use Snapchat. Being the pioneer of vertical mobile video, Snapchat is the ideal platform for attracting traffic to your website. Encourage sharing of videos and photos on your site, and share excellent Stories, make sure your content is up to date and make sure you post the most recent business or brand innovations.

16. Make use of the Direct CTAs (Call to Action) and create longer videos

CTAs are extremely effective marketing tools, and are highly recommended for Snapchat as the platform allows users to respond to Ads swiftly. This is essential since what every company or marketer would like is for viewers to go to the next step to convert and finally spend money on the brand.

When making videos for Snapchat There are two aspects to be considered that is the orientation as well as the length. The ideal orientation is vertical, as the majority of people who are watching videos will do so using an mobile device. For length, think about creating entertaining and engaging long-form videos that are more effective within the short time frame available.

17. Utilize Snap Ads templates to make engaging video Ads

If you don't have enough time or aren't capable of coming up with great video Ads You can make use of Snapchat's templates to create your own unique Ads. There's plenty of options of templates to choose from, and the option of even more customizable options.

The templates are designed to conform to the desired orientation and are compatible the mobile device. This is a great solution for sharing content while on the move or for times when your creativity is shut down.

18. Utilize Shout-Outs from other accounts

If you've ever previously used Snapchat previously, you've seen users getting shout-outs from accounts of other users. The 'Follow my friend's profile message on a certain post of a user is quite extremely popular.

To reap the maximum benefit of this, you must find an influential user with a large following. There are likely to be acquaintances or colleagues whom you can request to let you know they're listening out and forward a few of their followers to you in particular on a article that's in your area of expertise.

Apart from acquaintances, you can discover well-known Snapchat celebrities who give frequent shout-outs. Contact them to post your content and to mention your username. The people who read the content might be interested in your page and check it again for new articles, and may even follow your account to keep up-to-date If they enjoy it.

It you don't have acquaintances who have a huge following, you may make a payment to have shout-outs. To get this done you must locate an influential person of high rank that has lots of followers and has high levels of engagement, particularly within your particular field or at a minimum closely related to in order to get the best outcomes.

The next step is to ask the person who is promoting your page by using your username, and then asking your friends to look up your page.

Once you've mastered the basics the process, Snapchat could be extremely useful to your company and can be a breeze to navigate around. Of course, it's not suitable for every company, but if you are aware of your company's needs and most importantly, your market, then you'll be able to determine if Snapchat will be a success for you.

19. Always evaluate progress and succeed

What can you tell if you're succeeding in Snapchat advertising or otherwise?

You must be able to test your marketing strategy prior to begin to implement it, as well as an approach to evaluate your progress to determine whether you're hitting your goals and assist you in making any needed adjustments or adjustments. It is possible to use Snap Pixel, a tool that advertisers can use to monitor the actions that followers perform on their sites.

These are the top Snapchat strategies and marketing methods that you can implement. They will create a following for your company and boost your brand's visibility on the internet.

Once you've gotten used with it Snapchat is beneficial to your business and can be a breeze to navigate around. Of course, it's not suited to every company, but if you are aware of your company's needs and, most importantly your market then you'll be able determine whether Snapchat is a good fit for your business.

Try out various strategies and methods Explore new strategies and don't be scared to think outside the box. The most appealing aspect of this app is the simple nature that requires less complex content. So long as your content can be a good fit with your audience, you're in good shape.

Snapchat is an established social marketing and media platform - it's no longer the newest youngster to be ignored. It has grown in the years since it was first launched with followers and growth; With more than 150 million daily users as compared to 5 million daily users in 2013 and they are increasing!

In the next chapter, we'll take a look at some Snapchat success stories in marketing.

Chapter 7: Snapchat Success Stories

Snapchat has been unfairly and incorrectly been seen by business owners marketing and other professionals as an brand new young-people's app for quite a while. Therefore, not many companies use it for marketing but that does not mean you have to abandon your efforts to explore the platform.

Actually, the attitude toward Snapchat has changed drastically over the last 5 years. The world is now aware that Snapchat is essential in marketing, not just due to the giddy features it introduced us the world features, but also due to the demographics of its users.

And, let's face the facts If your market is anyone from 13 to 34 and you want to reach them, then Snapchat is an absolute must for you.

Of course, there could be a few of you contemplating the rationale for investing on a platform that displays your content for 24 hours. Do you think it is worth your time and effort?

In addition Is there any other business that has really succeeded with this approach?

To help you answer your questions We have put together the following list of the companies who have used the platform successfully to promote their brands. There are a lot of companies there , but these are only few. We also have included the strategies they have put in the first place.

1. Gilmore Girls on Netflix

If Netflix decided to broadcast Gilmore Girls in 2016, they launched a Snapchat sponsored Filter campaign to announce its return to television and inform the viewers about Gilmore Girls' revival. Netflix released an Snapcode that was used to access the only Snapchat Filter to the revamped Gilmore Girls show.

Netflix collaborated with hundreds of coffee shops and cafes across America. US in order to create Luke's café in the show. They also provided 10,000 cups of coffee with an encryptable Snapcode to unlock the new Gilmore Girls. The Netflix campaign generated buzz and spread news about the show's upcoming premiere.

It worked well as the show's viewers queued in selected shops for coffee cups using the Snapcode. They snapped pictures of the cups , shared the pictures with their friends and allowed them to unlock the lenses, which led to more people being aware of the relaunch , and creating a lot of interest for Netflix. It was so effective was the Netflix campaign that it was seen more than 800,000 times by half a million viewers in just one day.

The Snapchat campaign of Netflix and Gilmore Girls was a huge success because it was entertaining and promised value with the free filter and the merchandise.

2. Grubhub

The company that provides food delivery has been embracing the application of Snapchat. The business relies on the mobile app of its customers for their operation, which means their customer base is tech-savvy users who can operate smartphones.

Their target market is likely to be users who are drawn to interacting via apps, the business utilized this information to expand their reach by extending the brand to the place where the majority of their customers hang out: Snapchat.

The millennial generation who make up a major segment of the market that is a target for Grubhub are using their phones more often than other people. With their smartphones most of the time on social media, which is a an enormous opportunity for online marketers.

Then, there's Grubhub prepared to make the most of this information.

They have set up extremely entertaining social media profiles on which they asked their followers to engage with their content. They've also held contests using Snapchat which have generated interactions between their old and new followers.

The platform has been used to offer original content that is appealing to people who use Snapchat who are predominantly young people. They have utilized Snapchat to enhance their relationship with customers and also have a greater number of people making use of their services.

The Snapchat campaign was successful due to the fact that Grubhub was able to target the right people and was one of the first companies to make use of Snapchat to recruit, which gained lots of attention.

3. Cedar Point: Haunt

Cedar Point ran a very popular contest on Snapchat to promote Halloween celebrations in the amusement park. Because Snapchat comes with an alert feature to notify users of the screenshot of their Snap, Cedar Point used this feature to their advantage to organize the contest.

By using the Snapchat Story where a ghost flashed for an instant within the Story, Cedar Point asked users to take a picture of the ghost that flashed before it vanished. first five users to get the picture were rewarded.

The ghost's appearance lasted just a moment, users were required to watch the video several times to get an image of it. Watching it repeatedly meant that they had to read the advertising message of the brand, however the experience also generated an increase in interest and the spreading the Story.

In this way, Cedar Point increased its engagement through Snapchat by more than 200 percent. It was a success largely due to the message resonated with Snapchat users particularly the younger generation.

4. Chubbies Shorts

This online retailer of shorts for men has one of the most effective advertising campaigns available in the world of e-commerce. Chubbies Shorts are a start-up that has embraced social media in its maximum potential by using Facebook, Twitter, and YouTube to advertise their goods.

The company offers vibrantly colored shorts for males. Who would be the most interested in this kind of clothing?

The younger generation is definitely the most likely target often called the millennials. Because of this particular target market, they decided to take their advertising to Snapchat also.

Chubbies Shorts is a company Chubbies Shorts was started by three college buddies at Stanford University in 2011, and their principal customers became others who were students at Stanford University. They're people who love to socialize online. Chubbies's job therefore is to make use of this information to create specific content for this kind of user.

They create funny videos that you can share on Snapchat. They're just like the hilarious person of yours who you want to spend time with, however, you are able to connect with them on the internet by watching their hilarious videos.

They also produce a short video produced each week, which they share every week on Snapchat. These methods aren't in any way linked to making instant conversions to sales. They're not trying to market their product at

Snapchat users, at a minimum not in a clear method.

The content they make is intended to entertain their viewers, and keep them entertained and eager to see more of the same type of content.

What it will do is create an increased bond between the brand and its customers, meaning when someone wants to buy a pair of shorts, they instantly imagine Chubbies Shorts. This is a tactful method to promote your brand and the results are astounding such as the one shown through Chubbies Shorts.

5. Gatorade

Gatorade made a splash with its sponsored Snapchat lens at the 2015 Super Bowl. Gatorade did a great job of getting the lens to stand out in light of the advertising competition and the innovation that took place in this year's Super Bowl.

In a nod to the usual NFL touchline ritual of showering the head coach of a winning team with drinks of the cooler on which they play generally Gatorade the lens set an invitation to American fans of football to snap selfies while bathed in Gatorade.

The lens was watched more than 100 million times. Sponsored lenses aren't suitable for everyone due to their cost, but brands who can afford them profit big by using them.

6. Casper

A mattress-selling business is likely not something you would are expecting on Snapchat you think? So, what can they possibly provide the users on Snapchat? How do they keep the exciting, fun content that is required of Snapchat marketing that is appealing to cool young people?

Mattresses are boring. You purchase them for sleeping on, and they aren't things you can take photos of and share with your family. They're not the most thrilling of items and getting youngsters to discuss it is a lot harder.

But Casper appears to have been able to discover something that very few companies have, making this platform function for your benefit regardless of the product you sell.

They know that the market that is provided by Snapchat is ideal for them as the people most likely buying a mattress sleep on are newlyweds or students who are planning to go to university, or young adults who are moving out to live on their own.

Because the target market is working with them, they came up with an opportunity to reach out to this market while remaining relevant. They couldn't simply concentrate on selling their product. They decided to market their emotions instead.

The company wanted to stand out to stand out from competitors , and to have their customers identify specific emotions with their brand. This is the way to attract the interest of the younger generation.

Casper does not market the mattress but rather the experiences that go with the mattress. Feeling the urge to binge watch your favourite series in an inviting, cozy bed or the relief you feel upon returning after a long day and falling asleep on your mattress to relax, Casper emphasizes on these sensations in their advertising advertisements.

They are focused on making sure that their viewers connect to their brand and come up with original material to achieve this. They are also regular in their updates, releasing every day new photos to ensure that their brand is in the forefront of the minds of people.

They also have a weekly series that keep their fans tuned in every week. They also host Waffle

Brunch Wednesdays, where the group goes to a new waffle breakfast venue each Wednesday. This keeps viewers coming to the same place every Wednesday to watch the show.

The idea behind the show is to give an atmosphere of relaxation for the viewers with respect to their beds. The show is based on the sleep habits of the viewers, and even the way that people sometimes want to get back to sleep after a meal that is satisfying.

Their frequent posts and their the ability to be a relatable brand make them a sought-after brand. They don't just post material on mattresses. This is sure to be boring in the type of market they're presenting to. Their content is relevant for the people who read it.

So, when people are in the market for an item for their mattress the first brand that comes to their minds is Casper.

7. Great Lakes

Great Lakes made use of another Snapchat feature with great success and also for the purpose of marketing. Utilizing customized Geofilters which are seldom utilized, Great Lakes managed to get over 20,000 impressions using the Geofilter which was purchased for $35.

Their followers were targeted and gave discounts that earned the company an average convert rate of 12 percent. This is an illustration of how effective Flash sales could be through Snapchat as the user was already engaged and all they needed was a discount that was offered to encourage them to purchase.

8. Wet Seal

The apparel company employed an unusual, but highly popular method for Snapchat marketing called Takeover marketing. The company is extremely appealing to teens, and that is the reason for its use of Snapchat the app, which has a large number of teenagers using it.

The company has utilized influencer marketing to make a mark on Snapchat. For example, it has joined forces with @MissMeghanMakeup, a beauty blogger and influencer with more than 300,000 followers on social media. She was the one to take the control of the company's Snapchat page for two weeks.

Megan uploaded photos of her doing her normal routine in The Wet Seal apparel. She mentioned the brand at least a couple of times and performed things that teens do in their daily lives.

The deal ended up with 6,000 people viewing the stories that were posted, and 9,000 followers added for Wet Seal. Wet Seal page. It was quite a outcome especially considering the fact that the company just launched in 2013.

This is a perfect example of how influencer marketing could benefit businesses that are using Snapchat for marketing. If you use it properly you'll be reeling from the benefits.

9. Kraft Mac & Cheese

The mac and cheese business also utilizes Snapchat for marketing purposes. It's an established firm. For one of its advertising campaigns they developed lenses that were sponsored by the company.

It was the period when they were just beginning to get rid of artificial flavorings, preservatives and dyes in their products, to make them healthier and sustainable. The lens was a kind of game in which users had trying to take mac and cheese noodles with their mouths. It was a very enjoyable lens that attracted quite several users trying it out.

Conclusion

Snapchat is a distinct photo-sharing service that allows pictures to be only accessible for short periods of time. While some might view it to be a dead end platform, the truth is that there's plenty to be gained through this platform, especially in terms of turning leads to customers. Snapchat has unique features that permit users to take their users through engaging daily experiences that let them discover more about your company and what you're about. Snapchat lets you send intimate photos to your followers, and offer them exclusive special experiences that you can not provide in other platforms. accounts.

Effectively making use of Snapchat to convert customers is by knowing the way Snapchat can be integrated into your marketing strategy the best way. You must know that Snapchat is best when employed as a component the sales funnel which is when you bring users from Snapchat out onto other social media accounts which you can provide them with more information in order that they are able to learn more about your company and also about the products or services you offer.

I hope this book will provide you with the exact steps on how to use Snapchat to effectively promote your business to your followers and turn your followers into customers who pay. Utilizing your imagination and imagination, and by posting frequently and encouraging people to check out the other sites and profiles, you can transform your followers to customers.

Next step, you must begin learning how to advertise to your followers in addition to building your followers. Be patient and grow your following accordingly. It is important to share valuable content that is consumable every day so that your followers can find out more about your company and you and also include call-to-action posts that lead people to follow your path. The more content you share the more you will be able to increase your reach. It is also advisable to begin making use of paid ads in order to grow your reach faster by connecting with a community that you may not have been able to meet.

As long as you stick to this advice and ensure that you post regular content and you'll be able the art of Snapchat marketing quickly. In the end, you can make a substantial amount of money by turning your followers to customers.

Thank you and best of luck!